FROM PROPHECY INTO HISTORY

Proof of God's Hand on the Bible

For Mom & Dad. Thank
you for your support.
Love,
Travis

FROM PROPHECY INTO HISTORY

Proof of God's Hand on the Bible

TRAVIS SWART

Carpenter's Son Publishing

From Prophecy into History: Proof of God's Hand on the Bible

© 2015 by Travis Swart

Published by Carpenter's Son Publishing, Franklin, Tennessee

Published in association with Larry Carpenter of Christian Book Services, LLC, Franklin, Tennessee

Cover and Interior Design by Suzanne Lawing

Edited by Tammy Kling and Gail Fallen

Printed in the United States of America

978-1-942587-18-7

From Prophecy into History *is an important book for those who want to know if the Bible, and Christianity, are true. Fulfilled prophecy is one of the oldest evidences given for the Christian faith, and yet it has not been as developed as other forms of apologetics. I am thrilled to see that Travis has taken the time to simplify and clarify the evidence from prophecy so both believers and skeptics can benefit.*

SEAN MCDOWELL, PH.D.
ASSISTANT PROFESSOR OF CHRISTIAN APOLOGETICS
BIOLA UNIVERSITY
BEST-SELLING AUTHOR, SPEAKER

When the missionaries and evangelists in the earliest Church offered up reasons for faith to a skeptical world their reasons almost always centered on miraculous acts and on fulfilled prophecy. The art of using prophecy as a tool of apologetics has not been used in many generations. And I am delighted to see Travis Swart remind us just how important prophecy can be in the defense of the faith.

CRAIG J. HAZEN, PH.D.
FOUNDER AND DIRECTOR OF MA PROGRAM IN APOLOGETICS
BIOLA UNIVERSITY
AUTHOR OF *FIVE SACRED CROSSINGS*

Travis Swart has given us a gift. In a clear and uncomplicated way, he's helped us see how fulfilled prophesy leads us to a deeper awe and trust of God's Word and the Author of the Word. For some this is a great review. For many it will open up a new world to the mystery revealed through the Bible.

GLEN ELLIOTT
LEAD PASTOR, PANTANO CHRISTIAN CHURCH

*This book is dedicated to my wonderful wife, Catherine.
Thank you for all your support and for hanging in there
with me over the last two years.*

*Special thanks to my friends and family
for your input and encouragement.*

*My sincere gratitude to Keith as well, who led me to challenge
my faith, which thereafter kindled my passion for serving the Lord.*

CONTENTS

INTRODUCTION

*"Go your way, Daniel, because the words are rolled up
and sealed until the time of the end . . . None of the wicked
will understand, but those who are wise will understand."*
—DANIEL 12:9, 10B

"**Prophecy.**" Many see it as mere hocus-pocus and vague predictions concealed in myth, legend, and religion. Most probably associate the word with visions of the future and often "the Apocalypse." Religions since the dawn of time have had their wise men, soothsayers, diviners, and prophets—all of whom have made claims to bear the revelation of their gods or spirits. We can probably think of a few headlines in our lifetime about "the end of the world" as predicted or interpreted from some religion or culture's literature. We always seem to be intrigued by such things, only to sigh indifferently as they come and go without any effect—after all, who is ever surprised that no one can really predict the future of world events? Many try and guess right occasionally—even the weatherman can get things right from time to time—but most fall flat on their face and are never right consistently.

But what if someone really could accurately and consistently predict the future of world events? What if many people already have? And, what if all these people have done so over the course of 1,500 years, all weaving their prophecies together into one big, coherent picture that lays out the plan of the same deity over the course of history? Would you listen to them and at least consider what they had to say? They would certainly have my attention. Would it surprise you, then, to know that such a thing has already happened, and that events foretold by these prophets have repeatedly come to pass and continue to do so to this day? These prophets are none other than those of the Holy Bible. Nonsense, you say! All I ask is for a bit of your time to show you, then you can decide for yourself.

No other religion boasts the type of rich, robust, and accurate predictive prophecy like that of Christianity (which includes all of the Old Testament writings of Judaism). Both Old and New Testaments combined consist of around 25 percent prophecy, with over one thousand instances of predictive prophecy (LaHaye 2006, 7). Many of which can be shown to have been fulfilled in history. The Bible is unique in this aspect. "It is the only volume ever produced by man, or a group of men, in which is to be found a large body of prophecies relating to individual nations, to Israel, to all the peoples of the earth, to certain cities, and to the coming of the One who was to be the Messiah" (Smith 2015, Ch. 1). Jesus stands alone among all other religious figures in having the support of predictive prophecy foretelling his coming hundreds of years in advance. No scriptures among any other religion past or present bear such marks of divine authority. The importance and significance of prophecy in the Bible cannot be overstated.

My experience with Bible prophecy was sketchy throughout most of my first thirty years of life. Although I became a Christian at a young age, went to a Christian elementary school, and grew up in the church, I had very little knowledge or appreciation for it. I'm sure I had read over many of the prophecies addressed in this book before, but I didn't know what they meant, their significance, or how to connect all the dots. I took them for granted, as I'm certain many church-goers do today. I haven't encountered too many pastors that give sermons or teachings focused solely on biblical prophecy—most probably don't think prophecy is going to put people in the pews. (My hat's off to Pastor Glen Elliot, however, who opened me to new perspectives). While it does get sprinkled in here and there, most of us probably go through our spiritual journey mostly ignorant of such things—if Christians know very little about prophecy, how much more so with non-churchgoers? I'll endeavor to fix that on both fronts with this book.

What I have discovered in recent years is that prophecy can have great power to impact belief in the Bible, and more importantly, in Jesus. This is especially true when it can be related to events confirmed in history. Jesus and the apostles of the New Testament (NT) certainly knew this to be true. Jesus appealed to Old Testament (OT) prophecy throughout his ministry to point to himself as the Messiah. Luke's gospel tells us that after Jesus rose from the dead, he walked with two of his disciples and opened their eyes to all the prophecies of the OT that pointed to his life and purpose (Luke 24:13-35). These two men described the impact of this revelation as causing their hearts to burn within them as Jesus opened the Scriptures to them—they were connecting the dots!

The apostle Paul, who first took Jesus' message outside of Israel, appealed to the OT prophets for support until his last days in Rome. Under house arrest, he spoke to a large group of Jews, and "He witnessed to them from morning till evening, explaining about the kingdom of God, and from the Law of Moses and from the Prophets he tried to persuade them about Jesus. Some were convinced by what he said, but others would not believe" (Acts 28:23-24). Yet so few today realize the persuasive power of prophecy to reveal the truth of God's Word.

Prophecy certainly changed my perspective on the Bible and its truth—it changed my life, literally! Several years ago, during a deployment to Al Udeid Air Base in Qatar (I'm active-duty Air Force, by the way), I had an encounter with an atheist who caused me to begin challenging my Christian beliefs. I began studying many attacks on the Bible, and came across some issues that I couldn't get around. I came to a low point in my faith and was on the edge of disbelief. Then, I had an encounter with God through biblical prophecy.

I stumbled across a prophecy in the book of Daniel, which I had read before but never taken the time to understand. It took me a while to research it and find all the pieces, but what I discovered shocked me to the core. This prophecy was so specific, down to the month and year in which historians placed the predicted event, that I knew there was no way it was just some best guess of a phony prophet. I knew from my research that Daniel had written this prophecy hundreds of years before the event it predicted, and he hit it right on the money. Specific and timely. This realization of God's hand on the Bible took me from near unbelief and restored my faith to something more than it had ever been—not just belief, but knowledge of the truth. I think of this moment as God's divine "slap" across my face to wake me up to reality. From that point on, I knew the Bible had to be true—this was strong, positive evidence! So now I give it the benefit of the doubt when dealing with tough questions or issues which bring its truth under scrutiny. What's more is that through this encounter, God rid me of a shameful addiction that I had struggled with for years—it was as if God affirmed my newfound faith by removing the desire for the addiction in an instant. From then on, God and his Word became my addiction. The answers have come, and my faith continues to grow, especially as I delve more into prophecy and how it has related to history. It's amazing and scary all at the same time.

It is this prophecy and others that I wish to share with you so that you, too, might see how they reveal God's hand on the Bible and thereby reveal its truth. Through this realization, I hope you will come to understand and appreciate the implications this has on our very existence and the future to come. I have written this book for Christians and non-Christians alike, although I've catered it to those who are unfamiliar with and/or skeptical of Scripture. For those of you who are followers of Jesus, I pray the coming chapters will encourage you in your faith and provide you with new information to help you share that faith with others. For those of you who are unfamiliar with and/or skeptical about the truth of God's Word, I want to show you some amazing things about the Bible which prove it was not written by just mere men. With its authors' repeated skill in foretelling the distant future, it could only have been written by men with a connection to the divine. It is my hope that you will come to see the Bible's Scriptures as from God and trustworthy. I pray that you will become familiar with what Jesus did for us and what it means to follow him, and that you will understand how our relationship with him impacts our lives in eternity.

There are so many issues and questions about the Bible regarding its validity that we could discuss, but I believe prophecy is the best place to start because it speaks for itself, and it is very hard to just explain away as coincidence. If we can agree that these prophets really did have God behind them, and that his hand really seems to be on the Bible, then we should be able to give it the benefit of the doubt when we encounter issues or questions which seem to cast suspicion on it. Concerns like evolution, the existence of evil, and various difficulties in understanding certain Scriptures will then have no bearing on its truth. What remains is simply to understand these issues more thoroughly and to see how they fit into the context of Scripture and God's existence. I will say, however, that I have been able to answer most if not all of those tough questions and issues. If you have such doubts, I believe the same will be true for you if you take the time and honestly seek to understand. Either way, you won't be disappointed. I have yet to find any concrete argument against the truth of God's Word in spite of trying very hard to find one.

It pains me that so many pass the Bible off as just myth or hoax with such powerful testimony to its truth contained right in its pages. And yet, without the right guidance, prophecy can be very difficult to navigate, even for someone who has been exposed to it before. So it is my goal over the course of this book to take you on a journey from unfamiliarity with biblical prophecy to a coherent understanding of several groups of prophecies which predicted major world events well before they occurred. In doing so, we will see that God really has been working throughout history and the Bible, and that he has a plan—a plan for the redemption of his people, Israel, of all those who come to call Jesus Lord and Savior, and of the very world itself.

Many do not and will not ever understand what the prophets of the Bible have written, but those who endeavor to do so are wise and will be ready for what is to come. In the words of the apostle Peter, "We . . . have the prophetic message as something completely reliable, and you will do well to pay attention to it, as to a light shining in a dark place, until the day dawns and the morning star rises in your hearts" (2 Pet. 1:19). Let me now shed some light on the mysteries of God's Word and his prophets . . .

HISTORY OF PROPHECY

*"Above all, you must understand that no prophecy of Scripture
came about by the prophet's own interpretation of things.
For prophecy never had its origin in the human will,
but prophets, though human, spoke from God as they
were carried along by the Holy Spirit."*
—2 Peter 1:20-21

We have to start with the basics. Before we can read and understand the prophecies of the Bible, it will help to have a general understanding of what prophecy is and of its purpose in Scripture. Then I will introduce some of these prophets and set them in their historical context and examine their individual purposes.

WHAT IS BIBLICAL PROPHECY?

> *Prophecy: Proclamation of the word of
> God regarding the past, present, or future*
> [My definition]; *the inspired declaration of
> divine will and purpose.* (Merriam-Webster.com)

In regard to Biblical prophecy, we aren't talking about mathematical weather forecasting or statistical predictions about the stock market or the big game—we're talking about **WORDS FROM GOD TO MAN.**

From Adam through Jesus and the apostles, the Bible gives account of God's relational interactions with mankind. Sometimes he communicated directly to individuals through voice, visions, or manifestations of his presence in a cloud or burning bush or human form. Other times he spoke through angels or prophetic messengers. Whatever the method, it's clear that the God of the Bible had a desire to be a part of human history instead of just watching his creation from afar.

People often think of prophecy as a prediction of the future. While this is often the case in the Bible, there are many occasions of God pointing out the past or giving instructions in the present. God used the prophet Nathan to confront King David of Israel about his past sin of murder to convict David's heart about what he had done. God gave directions to a man named Noah to build an ark so that he might preserve his family and the creatures of the world from the devastating flood that was to come. God used a Jew named Moses to convey his Law to the people of Israel. All are examples of prophecy. The kind of prophecy we will focus on, however, will be that of future events, or "predictive prophecy."

WHAT ARE THE PURPOSES OF BIBLICAL PROPHECY?

1. Reveal the reality of God and his hand on history and the Bible	• Prophecy is God's fingerprints on the Bible. By predicting the future again and again, the prophets proved that they alone spoke for the true God of the universe and that he is in control of history.
2. Reveal God's will to his people	• God regularly issued guidance and commands for Israel or individuals through his prophets. • Many prophecies lay out God's long-term plan for Israel, mankind, and his kingdom.

3. Bring about adherence to the Mosaic Covenant

- After the exodus from Egypt, the people of Israel entered into a covenant with God to follow his Laws.
- The prophets constantly called for Israel to return to obedience of this covenant and condemned their immorality.

4. Warn of God's judgment

- Throughout Israel's history, the prophets issued warnings and decrees of God's judgment for the sins of Israel and the nations around her. Israel was not the only nation who displeased the Lord with their immorality.

5. Show that God is faithful to his Word

- Time after time, God has made promises and predictions to individuals and people groups; time after time, God has fulfilled them in the Bible or in history thereafter. He has done this to show that he is a God worthy of our trust.

6. Bring encouragement and hope to the people of Israel

- In spite of God's judgment and punishment against the sinful nation of Israel, he continually revealed a plan of redemption and restoration of their hearts and of their nation. He promised the coming of a Savior Messiah, a new covenant, and a new kingdom.

7. Reveal the identity of God's Son, the Messiah

- God laid out a thread of prophecies throughout the Old Testament that foretold the coming of this Savior Messiah. It is the most important theme in all of prophecy.
- As we'll see, these prophecies drew a road map to one person in history and revealed his character and purpose.

There are more purposes that we could identify, but for the most part, biblical prophecy falls into one of these categories. We will examine prophecies with each of these aspects as we go through this study.

WHAT BIBLICAL PROPHECY IS NOT . . .

It's NOT a Crystal Ball or Fortune Cookie . . .

It was never expected that prophecy would provide Jews or anybody else with individual predictions of the future. While God did proclaim prophecies for a number of individuals like Abraham, Moses, and David in the broader context of the Bible story, don't expect to gain a personal fortune-telling out of its Scriptures.

Photos © Danny Smyth and Kae Horng Mau. Accessed July 11, 2015. 123rf.com.

It's NOT a *Grays Sports Almanac* . . .

While knowledge of the future might have benefitted Biff Tanner in *Back to the Future II*, prophecy is not intended to exploit the present or get a leg up on the competition.

It's NOT *Popular Science* or *Mechanics* . . .

Skeptics often mock prophecy and expect that words from an omniscient being should predict

the coming of scientific advancements and provide limitless knowledge of mathematics or medicine. What we must keep in mind is that God's eyes are set on eternity, not this limited world which will pass away. God is pursuing his plan for our redemption and his glory, not man's plan for personal advancement and self-exaltation.

THE HISTORY BEHIND PROPHECY

As we approach the prophets themselves, we now turn to the history in which they lived, prophesied, and ministered. Historical context is extremely important to understanding the prophets along with the purpose and meaning behind their messages. In order to get a firm grasp on the subject, we must go all the way back to the father of the Jewish nation, Abraham, and summarize some of the major events of Israel's existence up to the coming of Jesus.

History of Israel

ca. 2090 B.C.

God calls Abraham, the father of the Israelite nation, into the land of Canaan (modern Israel). There God promises him a son from which an entire nation would be born, and that out of his offspring, the entire world would be blessed. He also promises that one day, this nation would come to call that land "home" (Gen. 12, 15, 22:18; Halley 2000, 104).

1876–1446 B.C.

Abraham's grandson, Jacob, moves with his large family to Egypt to escape famine. Here, for the next 430 years, they grow into a large nation and are eventually enslaved by one of the Pharaohs and put to forced labor for the kingdom (Gen. 46; Exod. 1, 12:40; Halley 2000, 130).

ca. 1446 B.C.

The Exodus. God calls Moses, an Israelite who had once been an adopted prince of Egypt, to return and bring his people out of slavery. After God brings ten plagues upon the people of Egypt, Moses convinces the Pharaoh to let the Israelites go.

After escaping into the desert, God leads them to Mt. Sinai. Here, he presents Israel with the "Mosaic Covenant," which consisted of the Ten Commandments and many other civil, social, moral, and ceremonial laws. The Israelites agreed to enter into this covenant with God to uphold his laws. God promised to either bless or curse them based on Israel's obedience to this agreement (Exod. 3-20; Halley 2000, 130).

1050–931 B.C.

The Period of the United Kingdom of Israel. The Twelve Tribes of Israel elect Saul as their first king. He is succeeded by David, who establishes the boundaries and military might of Israel. He takes Jerusalem as the nation's capital. His son, Solomon, later builds the First Temple to God on Mt. Zion in Jerusalem (Samuel; Kings; Chronicles; Halley 2000, 213).

931 B.C.

Solomon dies and the kingdom divides into the northern nation of Israel and southern nation of Judah (Samuel; Kings; Chronicles; Halley 2000, 213).

History of Israel

931 B.C. (cont'd)

The succeeding kings of each nation immediately begin to turn away from God and their covenant with him. They lead the Twelve Tribes into worship of false gods, into conflict with each other and the surrounding nations, and into moral depravity (Kings; Chronicles; Halley 2000, 213).

722 B.C.

The bloodthirsty nation of Assyria conquers the northern kingdom of Israel and takes the majority of its inhabitants into captivity (Kings; Chronicles; Halley 2000, 213).

606 B.C.

The First Exile. Babylon, having since conquered Assyria, invades Judah and subjugates them after a lengthy siege of Jerusalem. They loot the temple and take the sons of many prominent families (including Daniel) to Babylon to serve in their courts (Date derived from Jer. 46:2, Dan. 1:1; Mieroop 2007, 276).

597 B.C.

The Second Exile. King Jehoiachin leads Judah in a revolt against Babylon. Nebuchadnezzar sacks Jerusalem again and takes around twenty thousand Jews captive in Babylon along with the rest of the temple's treasures (II Kings 24; Halley 2000, 266).

539–538 B.C.

Enter Persia. King Cyrus of Persia conquers the kingdom of Babylonia and asserts his rule over all its lands (Mieroop 2007, 287). In 537, Cyrus issues a decree that allows the Jews freedom to leave captivity and return to Jerusalem and rebuild the temple of God [Yahweh] (Ezra 1). This marks the end of the Babylonian Exile.

586 B.C.

The Final Exile. King Zedekiah of Jerusalem revolts against Nebuchadnezzar again and brings the wrath of Babylon against Judah. Babylon lays waste to Jerusalem, sets the city ablaze, and tears down every prominent structure to include the temple and the city walls. Four thousand six hundred Jews are taken captive from Judah after this final invasion. Only the poor are left in the land (2 Kings 25:8-12; Jer. 52:28-30; Halley 2000, 266).

516 B.C.

With the help of Persian King Darius, the first iteration of the Second Temple is completed in Jerusalem on the same ground as the first (Ezra 6; Halley 2000, 291).

444 B.C.

King Artaxerxes I of Persia gives leave and resources to Nehemiah to go rebuild the city of Jerusalem and its walls (Neh. 2; Halley 2000, 291).

History of Israel

Ca. 400 B.C.

Malachi closes up Old Testament prophecy and history. This is considered the last word from God to Israel until the coming of John the Baptist over four hundred years later (Halley 2000, 485).

332 B.C.

Alexander the Great invades Palestine, defeats the armies of Persia, and peacefully annexes the lands of Israel. He goes on to conquer the rest of the Middle East (Halley 2000, 508).

167 B.C.

The Maccabean Revolt. Enraged by the attempts of Seleucid King Epiphanes to purge Palestine of the Jews and their religion, a group of Jews led by Mattathias and his sons rises up against him. They defeat Epiphanes and secure the freedom of Palestine for a century (Halley 2000, 508-509).

63 B.C.

Enter Rome. Two rivals vying for the high priesthood in Jerusalem appeal to the rising nation of Rome for help. General Pompey responds and decides to resolve the matter by subjugating Palestine as part of Rome. (Halley 2000, 510).

30–33 A.D.

Ministry of Jesus

While the coming of Jesus did not mark the end of the relevance of biblical prophecy, this timeline presents the historical foundation for the events we will address in the next chapter. Now that we have a basic understanding of ancient Israel's history, we can better understand the context in which the prophets of the Bible ministered to the people of Israel. This will aid us to better grasp the purpose of their messages.

THE PROPHETS OF THE BIBLE

The Old Testament records the existence of around fifty-five prophets of God by name, though there were seemingly more in the history of Israel. The exploits of some, like Elijah, were recorded by others, while many of the prophets such as Isaiah and Jeremiah wrote their own accounts. It's not within the scope of this book to study all of them, but I do want to familiarize you with those whose prophecies will be relevant in the chapters to come.

Prophet: A person who is an inspired teacher or proclaimer of the word of God [My definition]; *a member of some religions (such as Christianity, Judaism, and Islam) who delivers messages that are believed to have come from God.* (Merriam-Webster.com)

For the purposes of this book, we will only be looking into the writings of these ten prophets:

• **Moses**	• **Jeremiah**
• **David**	• **Daniel**
• **Hosea**	• **Ezekiel**
• **Isaiah**	• **Zechariah**
• **Micah**	• **Joel**

Moses

Doré, Gustave. Moses Breaking Tablets of the Law. 1866. www.istockphoto.com.

Ministry: ca. 1446-1406 B.C. (Halley 2000, 129, 187)

Era: Exodus and desert-wandering

Purpose: Moses was born into Jewish slavery but grew up in the palaces of Egypt. He went into exile in the wilderness after killing an Egyptian slavedriver in defense of his countrymen. Many years later, God chose him to lead his people, the Israelites, out of bondage and to the land promised to their forefather, Abraham. God worked great wonders through Moses during Israel's escape to properly introduce himself to them and to the world. After the exodus, God used Moses to connect with the people, introduce them to his Law, and establish a covenant (the Mosaic Covenant) with them to uphold this Law. Moses then guided the people through their wanderings in the desert, through battle and strife, and eventually to the Promised Land, Canaan.

Message: Moses' message to Israel focused on worship of and obedience to Yahweh as the one and only God. He also issued God's commands for Israel along with words of blessing and future judgment if Israel broke God's Covenant.

King David

Cordier, Nicolas.
King David. Ca. 1600.
Basilica of Santa Maria
Maggiore, Rome.
Commons.wikimedia .org.

Ministry/Rule: 1010–970 B.C. (Halley 2000, 213)

Era: United Kingdom of Israel

Purpose: : King David grew up as a shepherd but came to prominence after slaying the Philistine Goliath in battle. He was ordained by God as Israel's second king and solidified their power and borders. By the end of his reign, he had established peace with all of Israel's neighbors. He had a heart for God, and so God made a covenant (the Davidic Covenant) with him that through his off-spring, a coming Messiah, his kingdom and name would be established forever.

Message: David embodied the idea of a warrior-poet. He wrote many songs of praise and worship to God, of prayer, lamentation, and penance. Embedded in these songs, however, was poetic prophecy—images and words that didn't seem to point to his own life but to that of this future Messiah. To this day, even the Jews recognize many of his songs as prophetic.

Hosea

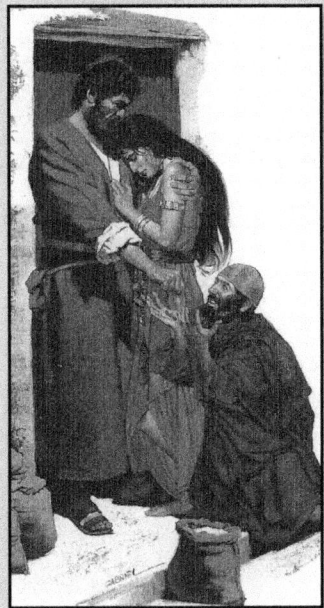

Unknown Artist.
Hosea and Gomer.
Accessed August 10, 2014. Psalm11918.org.

Ministry: Eighth century B.C. (Halley 2000, 446)

Era: Divided Kingdom of Israel

Purpose: Hosea ministered to the northern kingdom of Israel, whose people for almost two hundred years had fallen away from the Mosaic Covenant with God—intermarrying with non-Jews, worshiping idols, and living in moral depravity. God called Hosea to take unto himself a promiscuous wife to mirror Israel's adulterous pursuit of other gods and desires. Hosea's constant desire to care for and love her in spite of constant betrayal represented God's persistent love for Israel and his desire for their return.

Message: Hosea called for Israel to repent of their sins and return to the covenant with God. He warned them that they would be banished from the land should they persist in rejecting him, but that God continued to love them and foresaw the day that they would return to him and be restored.

Joel

Weigel, Johann
Christoph. *Joel*. 1695.
www.boomerinthepew.com.

Ministry: ca. 825 B.C. (LaHaye 2006, 276)

Era: Divided Kingdom of Israel

Purpose: Little is known about the prophet Joel except that he was likely one of the earliest writing prophets in Jewish history. His purpose is, again, one of warning, to call for repentance, and to offer a glimmer of hope for Israel's future.

Message: In spite of being one of the earliest written prophets, Joel's message pointed mostly to apocalyptic times far in the future. He foretold the coming of a massive invasion at which time he implores Israel to repent and turn to the Lord for salvation. The last chapter speaks of a final battle during which God himself will come to the aid of Israel and bring judgment upon the nations for persecuting his people.

Isaiah

Unknown Artist. *Isaiah.*
1904, Providence Lithograph
Company.
Commons.wikimedia.org

Ministry: 740–700 B.C. (Halley 2000, 366)

Era: Divided Kingdom of Israel

Purpose: Isaiah was a prophet of the southern kingdom of Judah during the period of Assyrian invasions. His purpose, like most of the prophets, was to call Israelites back to God and his covenant. During the Assyrian siege of Jerusalem, Isaiah's counsel to King Hezekiah led him to seek out God for salvation from their enemies. Then an angel of the Lord went out and destroyed the Assyrian army.

Message: Isaiah preached of adherence to the Mosaic Covenant and of judgment for not doing so. He also announced coming judgment against other nations for their persecution of Israel and for sinning against God. He additionally prophesied hope and the future restoration of Israel. The most important message through-out his writing is the encouragement that God would come as a Servant to redeem his people to himself.

Micah

Unknown Artist. *Micah the Prophet.* Eighteenth century. Kizhi monastery. Karelia, Russia.
Commons.wikimedia.org.

Ministry: 735–710 B.C. (LaHaye 2006, 287)

Era: Divided Kingdom of Israel

Purpose: Micah was a contemporary of both Hosea and Isaiah. He ministered/prophesied to both Israel and Judah, specifically their capitals of Samaria and Jerusalem. His primary purpose was to call the Jews back to God's Covenant and warn them of the consequences should they not return. He also addressed some of the social injustices of the poor and oppressed in Judah.

Message: Like many of the prophets, he preached adherence to the Mosaic Covenant and that the Jews needed to repent of their evil ways. He predicted the fall of Samaria (the capital of the northern kingdom of Israel), which he used as a warning to foreshadow the fate of Jerusalem should they continue in their sin. He later prophesied of Jerusalem's fall to Babylon, but promised hope in the future coming of a Messianic King and kingdom.

Jeremiah

Tissot, James. *The Prophet Jeremiah*. Ca. 1888.
Christianimagesource.com.

Ministry: 626–586+ B.C. (Halley 2000, 392)

Era: Pre-Babylonian Exile

Purpose: Jeremiah prophesied during the rise of Babylon and the final days of the Kingdom of Judah. He continued in the call of so many prophets before him—to cry out for their return to God and warn them of judgment otherwise. He personally witnessed the Babylonian sieges of Jerusalem and watched it burn before he, too, went into exile in Egypt after the final siege.

Message: He continually warned Judah of the coming of Babylon in judgment for their sins. He emphasized that Judah would be spared the coming wrath if only they would return to God's Covenant. He prophesied that Judah would go into exile for seventy years under Babylon. He also preached a message of hope and encouragement, in this case that a Righteous Branch (the Messiah) would come to redeem them through a new covenant and that Judah would one day be restored to even greater glory than before.

Daniel

Illustration of Daniel in the Lion's Den

Ministry/Service: 605–536 B.C. (LaHaye 2006, 219)

Era: Babylonian/Persian Exile

Purpose: When Nebuchadnezzar of Babylon sacked Jerusalem for the first time in 606 B.C., he took Daniel and many of the young Jewish nobility to Babylon to learn their ways and to serve in their courts. There, God used Daniel and others faithful to him to bear witness to his name in the heathen land of this new world power. At one point, Daniel was made ruler over the province of Babylon itself.

Message: Daniel's prophecies contain many specific and vivid visions of the distant future concerning the fates of the nations that would hold sway over the Jews, the coming Messiah, and the end of days. The overarching theme is that God is sovereign and in control of history in spite of the Jews' current circumstances. There is hope, God has a plan—history is going somewhere.

Ezekiel

Raphael. *Ezekiel's Vision*. 1518.
Galleria Palatina. Florence, Italy.
Commons. wikimedia.org.

Ministry: 592–572 B.C. (Ezek. 1, 40)

Era: Babylonian Exile

Purpose: Ezekiel was a priest of the Lord's temple who was taken captive to Babylon in the second exile (597 B.C.). Unlike Daniel, he came to live and serve in the countryside. He was a guiding light to the captive remnant of Judah, helping them understand the reasons for their punishment and calling them back to God as well as giving them hope.

Message: Before Jerusalem was destroyed, Ezekiel called for the Jews to repent of their wickedness and return to God, lest Jerusalem be brought to ruin. Of course, they did not, and five to six years later, that is exactly what happened. Ezekiel then focused on bringing hope to the exiles, proclaiming prophecies which assured them that God is in control and has a plan for the future restoration of Israel and for the establishment of his rule on Earth.

Zechariah

Ministry: 520–518+ B.C. (Hays 2010, 345)

Era: Post-Babylonian Exile

Purpose: Zechariah was a priest who returned to Jerusalem with the first group of freed exiles to begin rebuilding the temple. While he likely facilitated the temple construction, he was there, like so many prophets before, to keep the remnant from turning to old habits of wickedness and bring them hope for the future.

Tissot, James. *The Prophet Zechariah.* ca. 1888. www.artbible.info.

Message: While he warned the freed exiles not to follow in the disobedience of their ancestors, his message was mostly that of hope and restoration and that God had not forgotten his chosen people. He focused greatly on apocalyptic visions of war and on the greatness of Jerusalem to follow with the coming of the Messiah to institute his kingdom on Earth.

From this brief introduction, we can see that these ten prophets carry themes that are common throughout their writings:

1. God's care over Israel and all mankind
2. Obedience to God's Covenant and repentance of sin
3. Judgment upon Israel and others for their wickedness
4. Hope of a future restoration of the nation of Israel
5. The coming of a Messiah who will restore/redeem Israel and the world both physically and spiritually, and who will one day institute his kingdom on Earth forever
6. God has a plan, which is sovereign over history

Right now, some might be thinking: "Well it's nice that these writers tried to give some hope to a downtrodden people group, but they were probably just whimsical dreamers spinning and spreading false expectations of things to come." On the surface, this might seem to be the case; however, I will show you that these men knew exactly what they were talking about, because their words were from God. Interpreting those words, however, can sometimes be a challenge.

THE NATURE OF BIBLICAL PROPHECY

We also need to have an understanding of how the prophets operate if we are to be able to put the pieces of the prophetic puzzle together. While they do seem to focus on certain themes in their prophetic revelations from God, no prophet ever gives us the full story on any one idea. For example, no one prophet gives us all the predictions about the Messiah—they weave prophecy about him throughout each of their writings where it's relevant. They each reveal different details about his character, purpose, and about his coming to Earth. So it is with all the prophetic themes we will cover in this book—no one prophet has all the answers. This is why it can be so hard to read straight through a book of a given prophet—they all jump around and reveal different pieces to each puzzle. Keep in mind that the prophets were not novel writers—they didn't sit down and write all these things in perfect chronology. They were given revelations from God throughout their ministry, and they wrote things down as they occurred.

It will seem at times like *I'm* jumping around and using groupings of verses which suit my purpose, but this is not the case—I will be connecting the dots and walking you through the common themes throughout the prophetical writings. I am not in the habit of just pulling Scripture out of context and saying, "Haha! See what the Bible says!" So many on both sides of belief are guilty of doing this. I have done my best to consider each and every prophecy within the context of the chapter it is written and in the context of other Scripture which relates to it. Nobody can claim 100 percent accuracy in their interpretations, but context is what gives the best support. I shall do my best to relay this context to you as we go; however, I encourage you to dive into these Scriptures and see the context for yourself, as it would be impractical to quote entire chapters at a time.

Another difficulty in understanding prophecy revolves around the literary techniques the prophets use. Some of them are literal, some of them are metaphorical or like a riddle, while some prophecies were written in poetic form. Other times a prophet might rehash the same themes in a cyclic manner, revealing different details about the same theme or issue. I will highlight these and explain the logic of my interpretations when the need arises. Overall, I believe the simplest interpretation of a prophecy is probably the right one, and when in doubt, I use other Scripture on the same issue to help unlock its meaning.

Over the course of this book, we will examine predictions of a Messiah, judgment on Israel and the nations, and of the restoration of Israel and our world. We will look for their fulfillment in history and relevance in our lives today. But one last question remains before we can know if these men really did speak for God of future events: when did they put these prophecies down on paper?

WHEN DID THE PROPHETS WRITE?

This is where the prophetical "rubber" meets the road. I can't stress the importance of this section enough with regard to the prophecies addressed in this book. If we can't know that these men actually wrote of events before they occurred in history, then their claims of divinely inspired prophecy are extremely suspect and untrustworthy. (And therefore, I have no reason to write this book.) After all, such alleged prophecies could easily have been written after the fact, or future writers could simply have made up stories which fulfilled them. In response, I would say that given the scope and continuity of the prophecies and the history surrounding their writing, what we have on our hands, then, is the greatest hoax ever concocted by man. But of course, this is a possibility, however remote or far-fetched.

One of the popular theories in academic circles is that the majority of the OT was written during the time of Jewish captivity in Babylonia or perhaps later. The idea being that the Jews needed a story to justify their existence and give their people a place in history. Some argue that it was likely all just a compilation of myths and legends sprinkled here and there with a bit of truth. Others argue a later date for some of the prophets' writings because surely *nobody* can predict the future . . . So, while we could examine many responses to such theories, I am going to focus on the most direct evidence for the dating of these Scriptures—the earliest copies of the prophets' writings known to be in existence. And then we'll see for sure what events they predicted, if any.

The Dead Sea Scrolls (DSS). The DSS are one of the greatest discoveries in all of ancient Middle-Eastern literature, especially where the Bible is concerned. In 1947, a young shepherd boy tending to his flock near the Dead Sea went in search of a stray. Boy finds cave; boy slings rock; rock makes shattering sound; boy discovers pots filled with scrolls—and the rest is history. Over the next ten years, archaeologists discovered "tens of thousands of scroll fragments, representing over 900 different texts written in Hebrew, Aramaic, and Greek in and around the cave system of Qumran (Levon Levy 2014, "Discovery"). Around 230 of these documents are biblical. Partial or complete copies of every book in the Hebrew Bible, except Esther, are represented in the collection (Levon Levy 2014, "Introduction"). Several generations of Scripture copies were found, ranging from approximately second century B.C. to second century A.D. (Levon Levy

2014, "Background"). There are several methods which historians use to go about dating such documents.

The first and probably most obvious of these methods is good old-fashioned **archaeology**. By definition it is ". . . the study of ancient things, early times . . . it is the science devoted to finding and interpreting the material remaining of a place." It revolves around digging backward into the past, exposing different layers and the objects and materials within. Many specialists might be needed to analyze materials found, such as coins and pottery, and then compare them with other known dated materials to insert the new finds into their proper period of time. In the case of the Qumran caves, archaeology provided the timing of the historical context in which these scrolls were found by revealing when their surroundings were used or occupied. Archaeologists dated the Qumran materials from **second century B.C. to first century A.D.** (Vanderkam 2000, 20-22, 32).

Radiocarbon dating is a method for dating organic materials like the parchment and papyrus on which the DSS were written. Without getting into great detail, this method measures the ratio of higher-order carbon atoms, which all plants and animals carry, to that of the lower-order carbon atoms, which result from decay of the higher carbons when organisms die. Scientists can then work their way backwards in time based on the known decay rate of these atoms to figure out when the decay began (a.k.a. when the plant or animal died). While this doesn't give the exact date of the text, the gap between death and preparation of, say, a skin as a writing surface would not be that long (dead things tend to rot when not preserved properly). This method was used to establish a dating of a specific range of years in which the various DSS came into existence: **fourth century B.C. through third century A.D.** (Vanderkam 2000, 27-32).

The last and less-known method is **paleography**. "Paleography is the science that investigates the styles of ancient handwriting, that is, the ways in which scribes formed letters, evolutionary changes in those styles over time as a means for establishing a relative chronology of texts" (Vanderkam 2000, 22). This method, like the carbon dating, is useful for establishing a range of dates during which a particular writing style was used. It also considers other factors such as the type of ink and recording material used. In comparing the DSS with other dated instances of similar writing styles, paleographers have been able to establish the time period in which they must have been written. DSS expert paleographer F. M. Cross definitively established three periods of dates for the scripts found in the DSS:

1. **The Archaic or Proto-Jewish Period** (ca. 250–150 B.C.)
2. **The Hasmoneaon Period** (150–30 B.C.)
3. **The Herodian Period** (30 B.C.–70 A.D.)

Cross assures us that because of the rapid evolution of writing styles during this time period, paleographers can often date a particular style to within fifty years of absolute dates (Vanderkam 2000, 22-25).

Historians can then fuse these three types of dating in order to establish very reliable ranges of dates for the creation of the numerous Scripture fragments and scrolls which we are concerned with.

Now that we have an understanding of the science that goes into the dating of these scrolls, here is the hard evidence in print. The below table is the breakdown of the oldest Hebrew copies of the prophetical Scriptures we will be delving into over the course of this book. Note that "fragment" denotes partial representation of a given book. Each numbered fragment or scroll represents a distinct document from the others.

Dates of DSS Prophetical Scriptures				
Book Title	# DSS Fragments/ Scrolls	# Chapters Represented out of Total # in Book	Date of Fragments/ Scrolls fall in these ranges	# Fragments/ Scrolls from Hasmonean Period or older[3]
Genesis	24	34 of 50	Mid 2nd century B.C–2nd century A.D.	5
Leviticus	16	26 of 27	Mid 3rd century B.C.–1st century A.D.	2
Deuteronomy	33	34 of 34	ca. 150 B.C.–70 A.D.+	9
Psalms	39	26 of 150	Mid 2nd century B.C–50-68 A.D.	4
Isaiah	1 Complete scroll[1] / 20 fragments	66 of 66	125 B.C.–60 A.D.	10
Jeremiah	6	31 of 52	200 B.C.–late 1st century A.D.	2
Ezekiel	7	18 of 48	Early 1st century B.C.–70 A.D.+	2
Daniel	8	11 of 12	125 B.C.–50 A.D.	3
Book of the Twelve Minor Prophets[2]	10	63 of 67	150 B.C.–25 B.C.	10
–Hosea	--	14 of 14	--	--
–Micah	--	7 of 7	--	--
–Zechariah	--	12 of 14	--	--
–Joel	--	3 of 3	--	--

Table 1.2: Data compiled from (Vanderkam 2002) and (Levon Levy 2014, "Archive")
1. See sidebar on the Great Isaiah Scroll for more details.
2. The Hebrew Bible combines the twelve Minor Prophets into one book, and so they are all treated as together in this chart. I broke out our four prophets from the whole, so we could see how many chapters of their writing are found in the DSS.
3. These numbers are extracted from the Dead Sea Scrolls Digital Library, which does not include analysis of some fragments.

So, here we have it—definitive dates for the writings of each of our ten prophets. The earliest hard evidence historians have laid their hands on (save for a few older fragments here and there). A very good majority of chapters from all of these books is represented in the pieces of these ancient scrolls. Yes, some of the fragments for these books are dated after 1 A.D.; however, ALL of these books have fragments that are dated solely within the Hasmonean Period of Israel's history (150 B.C.–30 B.C.) or earlier (Leven Levy 2014, "Archive"). This means that every single one of these books was in existence before the time of Christ—and for the purpose and scope of our prophetical investigation, that's all the older we need them to be. So long as it was written beforehand, a prophecy is still a prophecy even if we can't physically date it as having been written when biblical scholars claim. (Although confirmed prophecy does lend credibility that the author was whom he said he was and wrote when he said he wrote.)

Based on the DSS dates and the arguments below (see "Arguments for an Earlier Old Testament"), I am going to assign an extremely conservative completion date for all these books by no later than **100 B.C.** I like round numbers, and this accounts for at least a fifty-year margin of error for almost all of the books' earliest dated fragments.

But wait! What about accuracy? The DSS might be old, but are they the same texts as the documents we have today? In short, yes! Most of the documents referenced above show very close similarity with the more recent Masoretic Texts (Vanderkam 2000, 104-39). Some, like the DSS texts of Isaiah and Daniel, are almost word-for-word identical (To be fair, some of the scrolls do have noticeable scriptural variations, which tie into other translations of the OT like the Greek Septuagint, but none of them change the overall meaning or original message of these prophets.)

The Masoretic Texts are a series of Hebrew manuscripts dated during the Middle Ages. The most prominent of these is the Leningrad Codex (ca. 1008 A.D.)—the earliest complete example of the traditional Hebrew Bible (Vanderkam 2002, 87). Modern Hebrew Bibles are based directly on these texts, so we can be assured that the DSS confirm the accuracy with which the Scriptures have been copied over a period of at least two thousand years.

The Great Isaiah Scroll

The Great Isaiah Scroll. Ca. 100 B.C. Photo © The Israel Museum, Jerusalem.

The most significant find at Qumran was a complete scroll of the prophet Isaiah twenty-four feet long! Historians have dated this scroll to around 125 B.C., and discovered that it is 95 percent identical with the Isaiah of the modern standard Hebrew Bible with the other 5 percent being mostly slips of the pen and variations in spelling (Archer 1974, 19).

It just so happens that many of the powerful prophecies we are going to explore come from this book—we know for a fact that all of its contents were written before Christ!

ARGUMENTS FOR AN EARLIER OLD TESTAMENT

So, are the Dead Sea Scrolls it? Are they the absolute, earliest bookend on the dating for the OT Scriptures? Absolutely not! There are many reasons we can know that the OT books were written much sooner than the DSS dates, even though we don't have many older hard-copy fragments:

Closing of the Hebrew Scriptures and Silence of the Prophets:
The last books of the OT that were written and recognized by the Jews
as divinely authoritative are Malachi and Chronicles, which historians
estimate would have been written no later than 400 B.C. (Walvoord
1985, 589, 1573). The Jews themselves believe that no prophets have
spoken since that time and that "the voice of God had ceased to speak
directly" (Ewert 1983, 69). No voice of God means no new prophecy after that time, which means that Jews wouldn't have been sitting
around making it up!

Dating of the Septuagint: The Septuagint is the original Greek
translation of the OT. After the coming of Alexander the Great, many
Jews around the Mediterranean region came to speak and read in
Greek. And so their Scriptures were translated to Greek from Hebrew
to meet this need. The earliest account of such translation goes back
to around 250 B.C., when King Ptolemy II commissioned the Greek
translation of the Pentateuch (the five Books of Moses) for the library
in Alexandria. Translation of the Septuagint continued from there and
was likely completed by 100 B.C. (Vanderkam 2000, 96). We know
that it was widely in use by the time of Jesus (Halley 2000, 527). It
goes without saying that if you are going to translate writings from
one language to the other, the original would have already had to be
in existence before this time period!

The Sopherim: Historical records exist of a tradition of OT scribes
called the Sopherim. They were keepers of the Scriptures from the time
of Ezra, a post-Babylonion-exile biblical scribe, through the coming
of Greece to Palestine (the fifth through the third centuries). Their job
was to copy, preserve, and teach the Scriptures (Jewish Encyclopedia
1906, "Scribes"). Since we have evidence of biblical scribes copying
and maintaining Scripture, then it's a good bet that said Scriptures
were already in existence by this time!

Relevance of Prophecy: If you recall, many of the prophets spoke
to the Jews in the context of coming judgment and destruction upon
Israel for disobedience to God. They fostered hope for restoration
from their exile and punishment and foretold the future restoration
of their kingdom. Many such prophecies about events already past

would have been irrelevant to post-exilic Jews resettling Israel during the latter half of the first millennium B.C. Making them up after the fact would have served no purpose. Jews take prophecy very seriously—The Law of Moses dictates that false prophets should be killed if what they say doesn't come true! (Deut. 18:20-22). The reason they are holding on to the writings of these prophets today is because they had proven themselves to be true prophets in the past by consistently foretelling events before they occurred.

Details, Details, Details: If the Old Testament had been concocted sometime during or after the Babylonian Exile, it would have been near impossible to recall all the historically accurate details of the pre-exilic kings, people, places, and events that have been proven in archaeology. There was no such thing as archaeology back then! The writings of the OT bear the marks of eyewitness accounts—details the original writers would have had to witness in their own time.

Horrendous History: Have you read the Old Testament?! Who would make up a history like that for their people?! The books of history and of the prophets paint Israel and their kings as mostly selfish and evil. The kings and the people are condemned by the prophets at every turn, and their country repeatedly crushed and ruled by other nations. Kings of that time period were not in the habit of documenting their failures and immorality. No one would invent such a history for their own people unless it was true to the way things really happened.

With all these points in mind, it's hard to imagine that the Old Testament was concocted at any time during the latter half of the first millennium B.C. All the evidence points to the fact that most if not all of the OT must have been written by this time. The Jews didn't believe any further prophecy had taken place after Malachi, so they wouldn't have been inventing new material after that period. There are several lines of evidence that suggest the Scriptures were already completed and in reproduction/retranslation by no later than 250 B.C. Moreover, the OT isn't something that the Jews *would* have invented after this time. Most of it would have been irrelevant and made for a history of their people that was downright loathsome and despicable. And finally, the authors seem to be so accurate in their accounts of history that it's hard to believe they weren't there to witness it in person! In conclusion, the OT has every appearance of being written and completed in the years prior to 400–250 B.C., and the DSS confirm that we have received these Scriptures very accurately.

Now, let's tally the evidence for dating our prophets' work. We have hard manuscript evidence that all of our prophets' writings were in existence by at least the first century B.C., with a number of them dating back to the second and third centuries B.C. We have further lines of evidence which give us bookends for the completion date of the OT, with arguments for 400 B.C. at the earliest and 100 B.C. at the absolute latest. A completion date of 100 B.C. for our prophets' writings puts them at the most conservative date possible when considering just the DSS dates and the completion of the Septuagint. While most of us could probably agree on an earlier date, I want to give the biggest benefit of the doubt to the most skeptical of readers. These prophets DID write down their prophecies before the time period of Jesus, and this is the furthest back we need to go to prove that the prophets in fact predicted many events of the future which have been fulfilled in history.

GOING FORWARD

Now that we've established an agreeable date for these prophets' predictions, I want to leave you with some things to consider as we go through these prophecies and compare them to history for fulfillment:

- **How is this possible?** How could all these men over the span of thousands of years have made accurate predictions of the future which all interweave and tell the same story? You'll see that their prophecies are not just random stabs at different future events, but that they describe the same events in different ways and details.

- **What are the chances** that these men could have just guessed without divine inspiration and been right time after time? We're dealing with probabilities, here—which is more likely and reasonable? Extremely lucky guesswork (many, many times) or divine inspiration?

- **If the Bible has gotten it right so far with these prophecies . . .** chances are it's going to keep getting things right about prophecies to come and that it's probably telling the truth about a lot of other things, too!

- **What are the implications for the truth of God's Word and for my life?** If it's been right about history (especially history before it happened), then it's probably right about its claim to be God's Word and its claim to hold the key to our salvation from sin.

We now have an understanding of the basic idea of biblical prophecy, we have the prophets and the history behind them, and we have an extremely conservative and agreeable date of 100 B.C. by which their writings were in existence and complete. Let us now open the Bible and the books of history to see if what the prophets predicted really has come true.

PROPHECY, HISTORY, AND A MESSIAH

"I bring you good news that will cause great joy for all the people.
Today in the town of David a Savior has been born to you;
he is the Messiah, the Lord."
—LUKE 2:10-11

Two thousand years ago, a baby entered this world under the most humble of circumstances in the unassuming little town of Bethlehem, just south of Jerusalem. Not much is known about his early years except that he grew up as a lowly carpenter's son in Nazareth, a poor town in the Roman province of Galilee. At the age of thirty, he appeared on the scene of history, heralded by his own cousin, John the Baptist. This man of humble beginnings went on to shake a nation and, eventually, much of the known world. He continues to move in the world to this day. No other man like him has come before or since. Today, almost the entire world knows his name—Jesus.

Since the very beginning of the Jewish faith, prophets have foretold the coming of a promised Messiah who would bless the nations and come as King and Savior of Israel and the entire world. God first promised this to Abraham and his immediate descendants, then through Moses, King David, and many of the prophets to follow. It is the greatest prophetical theme in all the OT. The writers of the NT gave witness that these prophecies of a coming Messiah pointed directly to

Jesus. Because of such radical claims from these men, Jesus has not only become the most influential but also the most controversial man in all of history. No small achievement for an impoverished carpenter!

How can we know, then, if what these NT writers claim is true? How do we know if the Gospels contain an accurate, honest account of his life and personage? We could fill a football stadium with all the books that have been written over the last two thousand years to explore these questions. But I like to keep things simple: prophecy and history. It's one thing for the gospel writers to make claims about Jesus and how he fulfilled the OT prophecies, but it's another thing if we can point to proofs that these claims are true. Jesus did exist and he did fulfill the numerous messianic prophecies of the OT. We can corroborate these facts with historical evidence from outside the Bible. Sound like a tall order? Let's see if the prophets and early historians can deliver on what the Gospels claim to be true about Jesus of Nazareth.

WHAT DO THE GOSPELS SAY ABOUT JESUS?

The greatest wealth of knowledge we have about this man Jesus comes from the four Gospel books of the Bible: Matthew, Mark, Luke, and John. They document Jesus' lineage: the events before, during, and after his birth; his early life; then, his later ministry, crucifixion, and resurrection. Thereafter, we learn more about Jesus and his purpose from the "Epistles" or "Letters" that his apostles wrote to different churches and audiences over the course of the first century A.D. The Gospels are our starting point, however, so let's see what these four writers claim to be true of Jesus.

The gospel writers gave testimony that:

1. Jesus was a very influential man, considered by some to be the foretold king

Men dropped their livelihoods at Jesus' calling:

"As Jesus was walking beside the Sea of Galilee, he saw two brothers, Simon called Peter and his brother Andrew. They were casting a net

> *into the lake, for they were fishermen.*
> *'Come, follow me,' Jesus said, 'and I will send you out to fish*
> *for people.' At once they left their nets and followed him."*
> – MATTHEW 4:18-20

> *"As Jesus went on from there, he saw a man named*
> *Matthew sitting at the tax collector's booth.*
> *'Follow me,' he told him, and Matthew got up and followed him."*
> – MATTHEW 9:9

The masses followed him and wanted to make him king:

> *"Jesus crossed to the far shore of the Sea of Galilee (that is, the Sea of*
> *Tiberias), and a great crowd of people followed him because they saw*
> *the signs he had performed by healing the sick . . . about five thousand*
> *men were there . . . After the people saw the sign Jesus performed, they*
> *began to say, "Surely this is the Prophet who is to come into the world."*
> *Jesus, knowing that they intended to come and make him*
> *king by force, withdrew again to a mountain by himself."*
> – JOHN 6:1-2, 10, 14-15

His influence carried on through his apostles after his ascension to heaven:

> *"Peter replied, 'Repent and be baptized, every one of you, in the name*
> *of Jesus Christ for the forgiveness of your sins. And you will receive the*
> *gift of the Holy Spirit . . .' Those who accepted his message were bap-*
> *tized, and about three thousand were added to their number that day."*
> – ACTS 2:38, 41

2. He lived a wise and sinless life

Jesus claimed to only do right in the eyes of God:

> *"So Jesus said . . . 'I do nothing on my own but speak just what the*
> *Father has taught me. The one who sent me is with me; he has not left*
> *me alone, for I always do what pleases him.'"*
> – JOHN 8:28-29

49

Jesus suffered direct temptation from Satan before he began his ministry and resisted him at every turn (Matt. 4:1-11).

The apostle Paul later affirms Jesus' sinless nature:

> *"Therefore, since we have a great high priest who has ascended into heaven, Jesus the Son of God, let us hold firmly to the faith we profess. For we do not have a high priest who is unable to empathize with our weaknesses, but we have one who has been tempted in every way, just as we are—yet he did not sin."*
> – HEBREWS 4:14-15

> *"And Jesus grew in wisdom and stature, and in favor with God and man."*
> – LUKE 2:52

3. Jesus was and is God in the flesh: the Son of God

John described Jesus as the incarnate "Word of God":

> *"In the beginning was the Word, and the Word was with God, and the Word was God. He was with God in the beginning . . . The Word became flesh and made his dwelling among us. We have seen his glory, the glory of the one and only Son, who came from the Father, full of grace and truth."*
> – JOHN 1:1-2, 14 (EMPHASIS MINE)

> *"Jesus answered . . . 'I and the Father are one.' Again his Jewish opponents picked up stones to stone him, but Jesus said to them, 'I have shown you many good works from the Father. For which of these do you stone me?' 'We are not stoning you for any good work,' they replied, 'but for blasphemy, because you, a mere man, claim to be God.'"*
> – JOHN 10:30-33 (EMPHASIS MINE)

He was worshipped as such . . .

> *"On coming to the house, they [the three Magi] saw the child [Jesus] with his mother Mary, and they bowed down and worshiped him."*
> – MATTHEW 2:11 (BRACKETS MINE)

"And when they climbed into the boat [Jesus and Peter], the wind died down. Then those who were in the boat worshiped him, saying, 'Truly you are the Son of God.'"
– MATTHEW 14:32-33 (BRACKETS MINE)

4. He performed many miracles as proof of this

"News about him [Jesus] spread all over Syria, and people brought to him all who were ill with various diseases, those suffering severe pain, the demon-possessed, those having seizures, and the paralyzed; and he healed them."
– MATTHEW 4:24 (BRACKETS MINE)

"Jesus, once more deeply moved, came to the tomb . . . Jesus called in a loud voice, 'Lazarus, come out!' The dead man came out, his hands and feet wrapped with strips of linen, and a cloth around his face . . . "
– JOHN 11:38, 43-44

5. He was crucified for our sins during the eve of Passover under Pontius Pilate so that we might be saved and have eternal life if we believe in him

"It was the day of <u>Preparation of the Passover</u> . . . Finally <u>Pilate</u> handed him over to them to be crucified. So the soldiers took charge of Jesus. Carrying his own cross, he went out to the place of the Skull (which in Aramaic is called Golgotha). <u>There they crucified him</u>, and with him two others—one on each side and Jesus in the middle."
– JOHN 19:14, 16-18 (EMPHASIS MINE)

"For God so loved the world that he gave his one and only Son, that whoever believes in him shall not perish but have eternal life. For God did not send his Son into the world to condemn the world, but to save the world through him. Whoever believes in him is not condemned, but whoever does not believe stands condemned already because they have not believed in the name of God's one and only Son."
– JOHN 3:16-17

Peter, one of Jesus' closest apostles, spoke even more plainly about this idea in his epistle:

> *"He, himself, bore our sins in his body on the cross, so that we might die to sins and live for righteousness; by his wounds you have been healed."*
> – 1 PETER 2:24

- Passover is one of the most important holidays of the Jewish faith, celebrating the events surrounding the Exodus from slavery in Egypt. Every year, Jews from all over the country would come to Jerusalem to celebrate the great feast.

- Pontius Pilate was the Roman prefect (governor) of Judea from 26–36 A.D. Judea was the Roman/Greek translation for "Judah," which was the southern half of the divided kingdom of Israel before the Babylonian exile.

6. He rose from the dead on the third day after his crucifixion

> *"Now it was the day of Preparation [Friday before the Passover holiday], and the next day was to be a special Sabbath [Saturday] ... Early on the first day of the week [Sunday] . . . Mary Magdalene went to the tomb and saw that the stone had been removed from the entrance . . . she turned around and saw Jesus standing there, but she did not realize that it was Jesus . . ."*
> – JOHN 19:31; 20:1, 14 (BRACKETS MINE)

- It's important to know that after his resurrection, Jesus appeared to many people over the course of forty days to include his family, the apostles, and around five hundred others (Matt. 28; Mark 16; Luke 24; John 20-21; Acts 1; 1 Cor. 15:1-11). He did this to prove fulfillment of the Scriptures, prove his humanity by showing them his scars, to prove his divinity in that death had no power over him, and to prepare them for their ministry to come.

- When his time on Earth was complete, he ascended to heaven to sit at the right hand of God and receive his reward of authority and power over heaven and earth for making the ultimate sacrifice for our sins (Mark 16:19-20; Luke 22:68; Acts 1, 2:33). He did this promising that he would one day return for all believers.

7. His gospel would be preached across the world

"And this gospel of the kingdom will be preached in the whole world as a testimony to all nations, and then the end will come."
– MATTHEW 24:14

- The word "gospel" basically means "good news." In regards to Jesus, it is the message of his life, death, and resurrection and his purpose for all these things. By his coming, he brought the spiritual "kingdom of heaven" with him. Those who choose to obey Jesus and accept him as Lord and Savior become citizens of this kingdom through the indwelling of God's Holy Spirit.

- Here, Jesus was telling his disciples that this good news would be shared across the whole world as a testimony to his name and sacrifice, and as an offering of salvation to mankind.

These are the biggest claims of the Gospels. They attest to who Jesus was/is and to what he came into this world to do. These points contain the foundational ideas behind all of Christianity. Pretty radical notions for anyone to accept, right? These gospel writers claimed that God himself came down to be amongst his creation and walk with us, serve us, and die for us in order to reestablish our lost relationship with him. Along the way, he performed supernatural wonders of power to include coming back to life!

So was this some phony story concocted by religious zealots or perhaps by the Christian church hundreds of years later? Or can we know these details of Jesus' life and what his early followers believed about him from other non-Christian sources outside the Bible? Keep the above seven points in mind as we dig deeper into the history books to answer these questions.

The Trinity. Another important concept about Jesus is the idea of the Trinity. The gospel writers revealed that he is one of three aspects or personages of God—he was not a separate god unto himself, but an extension of "God the Father." The three personages are "God the Father" (infinite in size, knowledge, and power), "God the Son" (Jesus), and "God the Holy Spirit" (the manifestation of God's power and love). All three are part of the same being, but serve different roles. A good, but not perfect, analogy would be that of our sun. The sun is a whole entity with several aspects: There is the physical essence of the sun, with its energy-producing properties (God the Father), and from it emanates both light (Jesus) and heat (the Holy Spirit). These are all part of the same entity and have their individual roles, but each cannot exist without the other. God the Father is the driving force behind the other two; the light (Jesus) is what we see (rather have seen), and the heat (The Holy Spirit) is what we feel when connected with God. Of course, this is only an illustration. God is not a physical or finite thing, but I hope you get the general idea. This will be important to understanding Jesus and the Holy Spirit throughout the rest of the book.

WHAT DOES NON-BIBLICAL HISTORY SAY ABOUT JESUS?

Any good skeptic would call into question the radical claims made by these gospel writers about Jesus. After all, they had a religious agenda to push, right? And who would believe in all this supernatural nonsense anyway? Well, what does it mean for the truth of the Gospels' claims, then, if all seven of them can be supported or verified by other neutral or hostile sources? I'll put it this way: these are the kinds of evidences that win court cases—and right now, we've got the above claims of the Gospels on trial. Next, we will look at seven of the most convincing such sources dating from the first and second centuries A.D., which provide details about Jesus' life and of early Christianity. Let's have our seven witnesses take the stand and give their testimony.

Flavius Josephus

Unknown Artist. *Flavius Josephus.*
Accessed August 15, 2014. Commons.
wikimedia.org..

Lived: ca. 37–100 A.D.

Background: Josephus grew up as a talented Jewish scholar who eventually became a Pharisee (a fundamentalist Jewish religious faction). He went on to become leader of the Jewish forces of Galilee during the Great Revolt against Rome in 66 A.D. He was taken prisoner by Vespasian, the general of Rome's forces, but found favor with him and was eventually freed. He bore witness to many other battles and events during the war and often acted as mediator with his fellow Jews. He later took up the mantle of historian and published several works.

Cited Works:

Concerning the Jewish War (ca. 76–79 A.D.)
–Account of the Jewish-Roman War

Antiquities of the Jews (93 A.D.)
–Secular and biblical history of the Jewish nation
(Jewish Encyclopedia 1906, "Josephus")

Testimony of Josephus . . .

"At this time there was a <u>wise man who was called Jesus</u>. And his conduct was good and [he] was known to be <u>virtuous</u>. <u>Many people from among the Jews and other nations became his disciples</u>. <u>Pilate condemned him to be crucified</u> and to die. And those who had become his disciples did not abandon his discipleship. They reported that <u>he had appeared to them three days after his crucifixion</u> and that he was alive;

> *accordingly, he was <u>perhaps the messiah</u> concerning*
> *whom the prophets have recounted wonders."*
> – JOSEPHUS, *A.J.*, 18.3.3 (BRACKETS AND EMPHASIS MINE)

In reference to the Jewish High Priest, Ananias:

> *"He assembled the sanhedrim of judges, and brought before*
> *them <u>the brother of Jesus, who was called Christ</u>, whose name was*
> *<u>James</u>, and some others, [or, some of his companions];*
> *and when he had formed an accusation against them as breakers*
> *of the law, he delivered them to be stoned."*
> – JOSEPHUS, *A.J.*, 20.9.1 (BRACKETS AND EMPHASIS MINE)

Here we have testimony from a pious Jew that Jesus really existed. Look at all the NT facts he confirms:

- Jesus was wise and virtuous

- Jesus was crucified under Pilate

- He gained many followers throughout the nations

- They believed Jesus had risen from the dead and was the promised Messiah, the Christ

- Jesus had a brother named James, who was leader of the Jerusalem church

This is solid, unembellished testimony from a man who lived and grew up during the time of the apostles when Christianity was spreading like wildfire. These facts and beliefs are supported by a witness who lived within one generation of Jesus' life—they were not concocted centuries later through legend.

The first quote is actually the most conservative version about Jesus found in a tenth-century Arabic manuscript (Pines 1971, 5). The most widely recognized version (evidenced by manuscripts as early as fourth century A.D.) admits to his miracles and more directly asserts that Jesus was the Christ (Pines 1971, 16, 70). I chose to use this version because, while more rare among the manuscripts and quotations we have of this quote, it gives the benefit of the doubt to the skeptic. Just one witness is not enough, however—let's call in the next!

Publius Tacitus

Lived: 56–ca. 120 A.D.

Background: Roman orator, public official, and historian. He was well-educated and served in various political and administrative roles to include governor of Britain, commander of a legion, and administrator of a religious college. He was a prestigious historian who wrote several works on the history of the Roman Empire.

Statue of Tacitus, Parliament building, Vienna, Austria. Accessed August 15, 2014. Commons. wikimedia.org..

Cited Works:
The Annals (ca. 109 A.D)
–Roman history from 14–68 A.D.

(Britannica 2014, "Tacitus")

Testimony of Tacitus . . .

Regarding the great fire of Rome under Nero (64 A.D) . . .

"Nero fastened the guilt and inflicted the most exquisite tortures on a class hated for their abominations called Christians . . . <u>Christus,</u> from whom the name had its origin, <u>suffered the extreme penalty</u> during the <u>reign of Tiberius</u> at the hands of one of our procurators, <u>Pontius Pilatus,</u> and a most <u>mischievous superstition</u> . . . broke out not only in <u>Judea,</u> the first source of the evil, but even in <u>Rome</u> . . ."
– TACITUS, *ANNALS,* 15.44 (EMPHASIS MINE)

While historians have never settled on who really started the fire in Rome, Emperor Nero did not hesitate to blame the catastrophe on the despised upstart religious group called Christians. Christianity opposed many of the immoral values of the Roman culture and religion, which brought hatred upon its followers. The passage goes on to describe how Nero savagely persecuted them.

Here we see that this group attributed themselves to "Christus," which is short for Jesus Christ. Tacitus confirms Josephus' claim that Jesus existed, and that he was executed (crucifixion definitely qualifies as "the extreme penalty") by Pontius Pilate in Judea (procurator 26–36 A.D.). He further time-stamps the event as having occurred during the reign of Emperor Tiberius (who reigned from 14–37 A.D.).

Not only does this passage confirm major facts about Jesus' life, just as extraordinary is the proof that Christianity did indeed spread very quickly throughout the Roman Empire. In this case, we can know that the gospel had reached Rome sometime prior to 64 A.D.—only about thirty years after Jesus left this earth. The labeling of Christianity as a "mischievous superstition" only supports the idea of how quickly it spread, and how opposed it was to Roman values. The case in favor of Jesus and Christianity is mounting . . . on to the next witness!

Suetonius Tranquillus

Lived: 69–122 A.D.

Background: Suetonius was a Roman biographer and antiquarian of noble birth. Under Emperor Hadrian, he served as both cultural advisor and administrator over Roman libraries and archives. As such, he would have had access to many historical sources from which to derive his works. He wrote several works detailing subjects such as Greek past times, Roman spectacles, and the lives of prominent figures in Greco-Roman history.

Unkown Artist. *Suetonius Tranquillus.*
Accessed August 15, 2014. www.nndb.com.

Cited Works:
Lives of the Caesars (121 A.D.)
(Britannica 2014, "Suetonius")

Testimony of Suetonius . . .

Regarding Emperor Claudius's decree for Jews to leave Rome circa 49 A.D . . .

> *"He banished from Rome all the Jews, who were continually making disturbances at the instigation of one Chrestus."*
> – SUETONIUS 121. CLAUDIUS 25

Regarding treatment of Christians under Nero . . .

> *"He likewise inflicted punishments on the Christians, a sort of people who held a new and impious superstition."*
> – SUETONIUS 121. NERO 16

The first passage confirms that Christianity had spread to Rome even as early as 49 A.D. and was going strong enough to cause a stir. That's only sixteen years after Christ was crucified. **This is *huge* for debunking the idea that Christianity came out of legends surrounding Jesus—legends don't tend to spring up within sixteen years of a person's life with so many witnesses around. If these Christians believed such radical and rousing notions about Jesus, they must have had very tangible reasons for doing so.**

Again, this author refers to Jesus as "Chrestus," or Christ. Given that this was written after Jesus left this earth, he could not have been directly responsible for instigating anything, personally.

> ## Dating Claudius' Decree
>
> The dating of Claudius' decree to expel Jews from Rome can be best extrapolated from events and persons described in the biblical book of Acts 18. Luke, the author of Acts, described this banishment of the Jews from Rome as having occurred during or prior to the service of Gallio as proconsul of Achaia. His service as such has been confirmed archaeologically and dated (ca. 51–52 A.D.) via the contents of an ancient inscription discovered in Delphi (Wake Forest University, Gallio).

Seutonius might have been referring to riots caused by evangelism to the Jews there. Acts 18 makes a brief mention of Jews reacting violently to Paul witnessing to them in Corinth just after Claudius's decree was issued. Such a response could certainly have happened in Rome, but we can't be entirely certain. The second passage corroborates the historical report of Tacitus regarding Nero's persecution of the Christians in Rome.

That's three witnesses, who lived within two generations of the coming of Jesus, who have affirmed some key biblical facts about him and early Christianity. I'd like to point out that the Roman writers are hostile witnesses to Jesus and Christianity, yet they confirm both the details surrounding Jesus' crucifixion and the early dates by which Christianity had spread around the Roman Empire. This means that they are very credible witnesses as to the truth of these facts—they had no motive or reason to make them up.

Lucian

Lived: 120–ca. 180 A.D.

Background: Lucian of Samosata was a Greek writer, speaker, and satirist. Born in northern Syria, he traveled west, where he acquired a Greek education in literature and philosophy. After much time spent travelling and speaking, Lucian settled in Athens and began writing critiques and satires of events and life at that time.

Unknown Artist. *Lucian of Samosata.*
Accessed August 16, 2014. En.wikipedia. org.

Cited Works:

The Death of Peregrine (169 A.D.)
(Britannica 2014, "Lucian of Samosata")

Testimony of Lucian of Samosata . . .

> *"It was now that he [Peregrine] came across the priests and scribes of the Christians, in Palestine, and picked up their queer creed . . . The Christians, you know, worship a man to this day—the distinguished personage who introduced their novel rites, and was crucified on that account . . . these misguided creatures start with the general conviction that they are immortal for all time . . . it was impressed on them by their original lawgiver that they are all brothers . . . [they] deny the gods of Greece, and worship the crucified sage, and live after his laws."*
> – LUCIAN 169. DP, 11-13 (BRACKETS AND EMPHASIS MINE)

In reading the rest of the context, one can see that this essay was not intended to be taken overly seriously; however, in his effort to mock Christianity, Lucian actually verified a number of key facts about it and Jesus, which are accounted for in the NT:

- Jesus introduced new teachings in Palestine.

- He was crucified for these teachings.

- His followers worshipped him and followed his teachings closely.

- They held that belief in Jesus as Lord and Savior granted them eternal life.

- The description of the Christians' close fellowship and morality is identical to that which we find in the book of Acts.

This passage proves that Jesus was worshipped as God at least as early as the mid-second century. This again supports the fact that Christ's deity was not fabricated hundreds of years after his death. This is a very significant fact, as many of these early Christians were Jews. Convincing Jews that a man could also be God would have been no small task. Jews believed they already had a corner on the one and only God and to believe anyone else to be a god was worthy of death. What teachings, then, could Jesus have been crucified for? Certainly not his teachings on morality and love—no, he was crucified for claiming to be God, which the Jewish leaders condemned as blasphemy! Little did many realize that he actually was God in the flesh. It would have taken a lot of evidence and persuasion to make so many thousands of Jews worship Jesus—especially in Palestine, the center of Jewish religion and culture. Perhaps witness of his miracles and bodily resurrection would have elicited such behavior? Perhaps his disciples performing miracles in his name? I mean, this was a poor carpenter who managed to convince his followers that he was God and Messiah. This was not some oppressive authoritarian leader who forced his people to worship him as some of the Caesars did or as certain modern-day dictators have done.

Another important thought to take away from this passage is *why* the Christians thought they were immortal. Christianity is founded on Judaism and looks all the way back to the book of Genesis for the reason of Jesus' coming. It was because of man's sin that God cursed us to die and separated himself from us, so only removal of sin can remove God's curse and restore God's original intent of eternal life. With this in mind, the reason Christians believed themselves "immortal" (and continue to do so) is that they believed something had happened to remove the curse of sin—that something was Jesus' sacrifice on the cross as a substitute.

One might laugh and say, "I don't know of any immortal humans in this reality," but it isn't that Christians have ever believed they are immune to a bodily death. Jesus, in fact, told his disciples that some of them would one day be executed for sharing his gospel (Matt. 24:9). Christians from then to now believed in eternal life of the spirit (Rom. 8:8-10) and of the promise of one day rising from death into an eternal physical body at the second coming of Jesus (1 Cor. 15:35-54). Jesus' promise of eternal life guaranteed salvation from the "second death" described in Revelation 21.

The Mishnah

Lived: First–Second Centuries A.D.

Background: The Mishnah is "the first written account of the early Jewish oral tradition and the earliest significant work of Rabbinic Judaism." These oral laws expounded upon the Mosaic Law and were documented

on paper during this period by a group of Rabbinic thinkers and scribes known as the Tannaim. They incorporated examples and debates on many areas of human existence. The writings were edited and assembled into six books no later than 220 A.D. by Judah ha-Nasi. They form the foundation for the Jewish Talmud (Cambridge, *Mishna*).

Cited Works:
Sanhedrin Tractate 43a

Testimony of the Mishnah . . .

> *"On the eve of the Passover Yeshu was hanged. For forty days before the execution took place, a herald went forth and cried, 'He is going forth to be stoned because he has practiced sorcery and enticed Israel to apostasy. Anyone who can say anything in his favor, let him come forward and plead on his behalf.' But since nothing was brought forward in his favor he was hanged on the eve of the Passover!"*
> – Epstein, Sanhedrin, 85 (emphasis mine)

Who was this Yeshu? Yeshu was short for Yeshua (Joshua), which was Jesus' actual name in Hebrew ("Jesus" comes from Greek translations). The Tannaim were of the same religious factions that put Jesus to death, so here we have hostile witness from the Jews themselves as to several critical details about Jesus' life:

- They confirm the Gospels' account of Jesus' crucifixion on the "Preparation Day" of Passover, ("Hanged" was a shameful reference to being "hung" on a cross).

- They confirm the Jewish religious factions' claim that Jesus did sorcery (referring to his miracles) by the power of Satan (Matt. 12:24).

- Jesus was accused of apostasy because he was leading many Jews into believing he was the Messiah (John 11:47-48).

Another interesting aspect of this passage is that it initially says the Jews intended to stone Jesus, which was the appropriate punishment for apostasy under Mosaic Law; but then it goes on to say that Jesus was actually crucified instead. This adds to the credibility of this account because, just as the Gospels describe, the Jews did not have the authority to execute anyone under their own law—only the Romans had such authority, since they ruled over Israel. So the Jewish leaders coerced Pontius Pilate to condemn Jesus under Roman law, who thereby gave him a Roman execution instead. This is about as hostile a testimony as it gets—the very enemies of Jesus providing historical confirmation not just of Jesus' existence but also facts about his activities and his crucifixion.

Pliny the Younger

Lived: 61–ca.113 A.D.

Background: Formally known as Gaius Plinius Caecilius Secundus, Pliny was a wealthy Roman author and administrator. He worked in Rome's civil courts and, at one point, headed the military and senatorial treasuries. He is known for his collections of his private letters, which included addresses to Emperor Trajan and his replies.

Photo by Wolfgang Sauber. *Pliny the Younger.* 2006. Cathedral of St. Maria Maggiore, Rome. Commons.wikimedia.org.

Cited Works:

Correspondence with Emperor Trajan, Letters 98 and 99 (ca. 109-112 A.D.) (Britannica 2014, "Pliny the Younger")

Testimony of Pliny the Younger . . .

Pliny made the following comments to Emperor Trajan concerning the practices of Christians, whom he had been investigating and punishing. These facts were relayed to him by several who claimed to have once been Christians but had renounced their faith, some over twenty years prior (or they might have denied their faith out of fear):

"... [T]hey [Christians] met on a stated day before it was light, and *addressed a form of prayer to Christ, as to a divinity, binding themselves* by a solemn oath, not for the purposes of any wicked design, but *never to commit any fraud, theft, or adultery, never to falsify their word, nor deny a trust* when they should be called upon to deliver it up; after which *it was their custom to separate, and then reassemble, to*

> *eat in common a harmless meal . . . this contagious superstition is not confined to the cities only, but has spread its infection among the neighbouring villages and country."*
> – PLINY THE YOUNGER 112, LETTER 98
> (BRACKETS AND EMPHASIS MINE)

Emperor Trajan replied:

> *"You have adopted the right course, my dearest Secundus, in investigating the charges against the Christians who were brought before you . . . Do not go out of your way to look for them. If indeed they should be brought before you, and the crime is proved, they must be punished; with the restriction, however, that where the party denies he is a Christian, and shall make it evident that he is not, by invoking our gods, let him (notwithstanding any former suspicion) be pardoned upon his repentance."*
> – PLINY THE YOUNGER 112, LETTER 99

These letters further confirm that Christianity was already flourishing in the Roman Empire by at least the late first century to early second century A.D. If it is true that some of Pliny's sources had been Christians over twenty years earlier, then we have, here, evidence that Jesus was worshiped as deity by at least as early as the 90s A.D.—this is within one generation of his life on Earth. Once more we have powerful testimony for early belief in Christ's deity. Pliny's letter also confirms that these early believers followed a strict moral code, as Jesus taught, and that they regularly met to break bread as reported in Acts 2:42, 46.

Again, we have a written testimony from a hostile witness confirming the Gospels' accounts of the beliefs and activities of early Christians. Pliny was trying to root out Christianity from their Roman society, not to propagate it—we can trust that his testimony is accurate and truthful.

Mara Bar-Serapion

Lived: 73–256 A.D.

Background: Little is known about Mara Bar-Serapion, except what we can glean from a letter written to his son while he was in prison. From his writing, we can tell that he was likely a philosopher, and that he was imprisoned after the Romans subjugated his homeland of Samosata in 73 A.D. The only surviving manuscript is a copy dated to the seventh century, preserved at the British Museum.

Unknown Artist. *Mara bar-Serapion.*
Accessed August 17, 2014. En.wikipedia.org.

(Van Voorst 2000, 53-56)

Testimony of Mara Bar-Serapion . . .

"What advantage did the Athenians gain by murdering Socrates, for which they were repaid with famine and pestilence? Or the people of Samos by the burning of Pythagoras, because their country was completely covered in sand in just one hour? Or the Jews by killing their wise king, because their kingdom was taken away at that very time? God justly repaid the wisdom of these three men . . . the Jews, desolate and driven from their own kingdom, are scattered through every nation. Socrates is not dead, because of Plato; neither is Pythagoras, because of the statue of Juno; nor is the wise king, because of the laws he laid down."
– VAN VOORST 2000, 54.

This is yet another early direct reference to Jesus, for who else fits the description of a Jewish king, who was considered a wise man and who was executed by his own people around that time? (As we saw earlier in the Gospels, some Jews did come to see Jesus as their rightful king and wanted to put him on the throne.) It is apparent that bar-Serapion was likely not a Christian, as he did not claim that Jesus lived on after his resurrection. He was more likely giving a secular account of events he had heard. Nevertheless, this is still early testimony to Jesus' existence. The fact that he held Jesus on par with other wise men puts him in great esteem as an influential man. As a secondary observation, bar-Serapion also corroborates other historical accounts about the dispersion of the Jews from Palestine by the Romans in the early centuries A.D.

Status of the Case. The first round of evidence in support of the Gospels has been presented. We have two neutral and five hostile witnesses who testified out of history regarding the life of Jesus and the lives and beliefs of his followers thereafter. Most of these sources date to within one to two generations of Jesus' life. That's early enough to know that the apostles and other eyewitnesses to Jesus' ministry would still have been alive to ensure continuity of the truth. Let's break down the major facts which these witnesses attest to:

1. **There existed a very influential man named Jesus (a.k.a. Christ), whom some considered to be the Jewish King and Messiah.**

2. **He lived a wise and virtuous life.**

3. **His followers believed him to be God in the flesh, the Messiah, and worshipped him as such.**

4. **His enemies acknowledged that he performed unusual feats they called "sorcery" (miracles).**

5. **He was crucified in Palestine under Pontius Pilate (26–36 A.D.) during the reign of Tiberius Caesar (14–37 A.D.) at Passover in the month of Nisan (March–April).**
   • **His followers believed that he died for their sins, which brought salvation and eternal life.**

6. **His followers believed that he rose from the dead three days after his execution.**

7. Christianity originated in Palestine and spread very rapidly around the Western world; Christ's followers strove to follow his teachings.

Look familiar? Our witnesses confirm or support all seven major claims made by the four Gospel accounts. In fact, even if we didn't have the Gospels' testimony, we could extract the fundamental beliefs and pertinent history of Christianity from these seven sources alone.

Make no mistake, Jesus was a real person and had a very real and powerful impact on the Jewish and Roman world (among other areas as well). So powerful that Christianity flourished against persecution and eventually overwhelmed the pagan beliefs of the entire Roman Empire without even having to rely on the sword to do so. We can also conclude that Jesus was indeed crucified, and that his followers (many of them initially Jews) quickly came to believe that he rose from the dead and was God incarnate. It'd hard to believe a dead carpenter could have incited such quick religious change in the world around himself unless some of these more supernatural beliefs were based in truth and the evidence for the apostles' testimony very powerful. In contrast, most of the other major world religions we know of did come about through legend and myth or were otherwise propagated by the sword such as Islam.

The case is looking pretty good, so far, for the believability of the Gospel accounts' major claims. We have numerous witnesses close to the events of Jesus' life and to the ensuing impact he had on the world thereafter. But can we have confidence that some of these supernatural claims are true? What if we have testimony to all these facts about Jesus and Christianity before they even arrived on the scene of history? I now call to the stand the prophets of the OT to show that the supernatural has already occurred in predicting these things and to act as a third line of witnesses to the truth of the Gospel events.

WHAT DO THE PROPHETS SAY ABOUT JESUS?

Now that we've reviewed what non-Christian history has revealed about Jesus after his coming, we're going to dive into what the many OT prophets had to say about him before his coming. We know with absolute certainty that all these prophets had their words down on paper no later than 100 B.C. I've already argued for earlier, but this is more than enough time to show that they could not have written all these things after Jesus' coming. While there are many more prophecies about Jesus written in the OT, I am going to focus on only those that we can verify as fulfilled through non-Christian sources (e.g., the seven major points we've been discussing).

1. There Would Be an Influential Man by the Name of Jesus (also called Christ), Who Would Be King and Messiah

<u>ZECHARIAH</u> → <u>The name of the Messiah will be "Jesus"</u>

Before we can arrive at the proper name of the Messiah, we have to draw a connection from one of the messianic titles that the prophets attributed to him. Isaiah, Jeremiah, and Zechariah referred to the Messiah as *"the Branch"*:

> *"A shoot will come up from the stump of Jesse; from his roots a <u>Branch</u> will bear fruit. The Spirit of the Lord will rest on him . . . "*
> – ISAIAH 11:1-2 (EMPHASIS MINE)

- This is telling us the lineage of the Messiah coming from the line of Jesse (father of King David), comparing the Messiah to a fruit-bearing branch of the family tree.

- We can also see that this individual will be closely connected to God through His spirit.

> *"The days are coming," declares the Lord, "when I will raise up for David a righteous <u>Branch</u>, a King who will reign wisely . . . He will be called: The Lord Our Righteous Savior."*
> – JEREMIAH 23:5-6 (EMPHASIS MINE)

- Here we have confirmation that the Messiah will come out of the lineage of King David as a "righteous branch."
- Note that this "Branch" will be a king called "the Lord" and "Savior." "The Lord" in the original Hebrew is "Yahweh," the proper Jewish name for God (QBible 2015). So this king was to quite literally be God in the flesh. Definitely attributes of a powerful figure. We'll come back to this part of the prophecy later.

In a vision to Zechariah of High Priest Joshua, an angel of the Lord said:

> *"Listen, High Priest Joshua, you and your associates*
> *seated before you, who are men symbolic of things to come:*
> *I am going to bring my servant, the Branch."*
> – ZECHARIAH 3:8 (EMPHASIS MINE)

- Joshua was the high priest in the temple after the Jews had been released from Persian captivity to go rebuild it.
- Here we see the Messiah described as both God's "Servant" and as "the Branch."

It's clear that one of the prophetic titles of this Messiah was "the Branch." Now let's draw the connection to the actual name of the Messiah revealed through one of Zechariah's other prophecies.

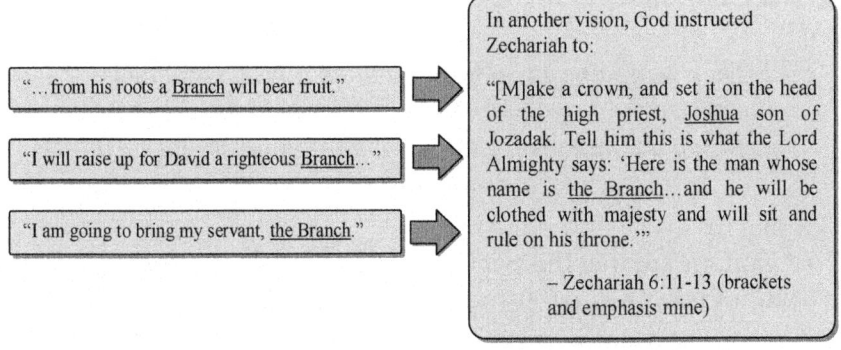

"...from his roots a Branch will bear fruit."

"I will raise up for David a righteous Branch..."

"I am going to bring my servant, the Branch."

In another vision, God instructed Zechariah to:

"[M]ake a crown, and set it on the head of the high priest, Joshua son of Jozadak. Tell him this is what the Lord Almighty says: 'Here is the man whose name is the Branch...and he will be clothed with majesty and will sit and rule on his throne.'"

– Zechariah 6:11-13 (brackets and emphasis mine)

- Zechariah tells us here that the high priest, Joshua, was the namesake of this "Branch" to come, who was prophesied to be the Lord himself and a king.

JOSHUA = YESHUA = IEASOUS = JESUS

© Liz Lemon Swindle. *Christ in the Red Robe*
Accessed July 15, 2015. www.goodsalt.com

- In Hebrew, "Joshua" was "Yeshua," which was Jesus' proper name in Hebrew; "Jesus" was derived from the Greek translations of his name, "Ieasous."

ZECHARIAH FORETOLD THE NAME OF THE MESSIAH TO BE *JESUS*.

We now have the name of this coming Messiah from prophecy at least one hundred years before his birth. Once again, we also have prophecy that this Messiah will be King. The connection with Joshua as the high priest means that this Messiah would act as high priest as well—the one who facilitates our connection to God.

Isaiah → Jesus shall anoint and influence the nations

We can see from the above verses that this Messiah will also be called the "servant" of the Lord. Isaiah builds on this imagery of the Messiah as a servant and uses it throughout his writings:

Isaiah introduces us to the Servant, recording the words of God:

> *"Here is my Servant, whom I uphold, my chosen one in whom I delight; I will put my Spirit on him, and he will bring justice to the nations . . . till he establishes justice on earth."*
> – ISAIAH 42:1, 4

- Again, we see that this Servant Messiah will have a direct connection to God through his spirit, and that his coming has implications for the entire world.

Isaiah, recording the words of God:

> *"See, my servant will act wisely; he will be raised and lifted up and highly exalted . . . so he will sprinkle [anoint] many nations and kings will shut their mouths because of him. For what they were not told, they will see, and what they have not heard, they will understand."*
> – ISAIAH 52:13, 15 (BRACKETS MINE)

- Here, Isaiah predicts that the Messiah will anoint the nations and have influence over their kings as they come to understand the purpose and significance of the Servant. There are a number of examples of kings being influenced by the church. Here are two:

  † In 390 A.D., Ambrose, the Bishop of Milan condemned Theodosius, emperor of the Byzantine Empire, for killing seven thousand Thessalonians in retaliation for an uprising. Ambrose called on him to repent of his sin and denied him the sacrament of Catholic Communion until he did so. (This was equivalent of denying salvation.) Eventually, the emperor humbled himself before a large church congregation and asked forgiveness for his brutal actions (Shelly 2013, 103-104).

  Bloch, Carl Heinrich. *The Sermon on the Mount.* 1877. Museum of National History, Hillerod, Denmark. Commons.wikimedia.org.

  † A similar event occurred in 1077. Pope Gregory VII excommunicated Emperor Henry IV for his repeated interference in church affairs. Eventually, the emperor went to Gregory and stood in the snow for three days, begging his forgiveness (Shelly 2013, 190).

  † Each case is an example of how Christians believed that the pope could deny the salvation of Christ. The influential power of Christ's church over the rulers of this world (for better or worse) cannot be denied.

- As we will see, the act of Jesus anointing or sprinkling many nations refers to the cleansing of sin that Jesus' sacrifice brought to the nations.

NO ONE CAN ARGUE THE INFLUENCE JESUS
HAS HAD ON HISTORY WITH HIS SACRIFICE,
HIS RESURRECTION, AND HIS TEACHINGS.

We can see that the prophets really did predict a coming Messiah named Jesus, and that he would be influential to the world and considered a king.

2. Jesus Would Live a Wise and Virtuous Life

Isaiah, speaking of the Messiah:

"Righteousness will be his belt . . ."
– ISAIAH 11:5 (EMPHASIS MINE)

"See, my servant will act wisely . . ."
– ISAIAH 52:13 (EMPHASIS MINE)

"He was led like a lamb to the slaughter . . ."
– ISAIAH 53:7 (EMPHASIS MINE)

*"He was assigned a grave with the wicked,
and with the rich in his death, though he had
done no violence, nor was any deceit in his mouth."*
– ISAIAH 53:9 (EMPHASIS MINE)

- In these prophecies, Isaiah makes it clear that the Messiah, Jesus, would have a sinless nature.

- Isaiah 53:7 draws a direct parallel of the Messiah to the sacrificial lamb of Passover, which God instructed the Israelites to kill and eat before the final plague struck Egypt in Exodus. The

©Phil McKay. *Behold.*
Accessed July 15, 2015. www.goodsalt.com

blood of each lamb was to be painted on the doorframes of their houses so that the Angel of Death would "passover" them. God specified that those lambs were to be spotless and unblemished (a symbol of innocence).

- In like manner, the shed blood of innocent Jesus protects those who believe in him from eternal death and separation from God.

3. Jesus Would Be God in the Flesh

Isaiah → A child will be born who will rule the nations as God

We've already seen that this Messiah, Jesus, would be a king from the line of David, who would have worldwide influence and bear the title "The Lord [Yahweh] Our Righteous Savior." Isaiah built upon this even more:

Isaiah, speaking of the Messiah:

> *"For to us <u>a child is born,</u> to us a son is given, and the government will be on his shoulders. And <u>he will be called</u> Wonderful Counselor, <u>Mighty God, Everlasting Father,</u> Prince of Peace. Of the greatness of his government and peace there will be no end. <u>He will reign on David's throne</u> and over his kingdom, <u>establishing and upholding it with justice and righteousness from that time on and forever."</u>*
> – ISAIAH 9:6-7 (EMPHASIS MINE)

- We know that this child is the same king mentioned in the earlier prophecies because he is to be of King David's line, and will bring justice to the earth. The Messiah and this foretold child are one and the same.

- There is only one "Everlasting Father" in the OT—one eternal God—and Yahweh is his name. Yet Isaiah tells us that this Messiah

Bloch, Carl. *Transfiguration of Jesus.* Ca. 1875.
Commons.wikimedia.org.

child would be the Everlasting Father incarnate. The conclusion is undeniable.

THE MESSIAH WAS FORETOLD TO BE MIGHTY GOD IN THE FLESH.

As we've already established, this is precisely whom the early Christians believed Jesus to be. While Jesus was rejected by the Jewish leaders as King the first time, we will explore later that he will return a second time for his people to rule over not just Israel but the entire earth so that he might have a truly free, yet righteous kingdom brought to himself.

4. Jesus Would Perform Miracles

Isaiah → God will come to save Israel and perform miracles among them

God encouraging Israel through Isaiah:

> *"'Be strong, do not fear; your God will come, he will come with vengeance; with divine retribution he will come to save you.' Then will the eyes of the blind be opened and the ears of the deaf unstopped. Then will the lame leap like a deer, and the mute tongue shout for joy."*
> – ISAIAH 35:4-6

- Little did the Jews realize that God's divine retribution would first be poured out on his Son Jesus for their spiritual salvation.

- Now that we know Jesus was foretold to be God, we can link this prophecy directly to him. The miracles predicted here are only a sample of the kinds of miracles attributed to Jesus in the Gospels.

- What better way for him to have revealed his loving, divine nature than to wield his power to heal and comfort those in need.

ISAIAH PREDICTED THE MESSIAH WOULD DO MIRACLES FOR ISRAEL —HIS OWN ENEMIES, THE JEWISH RELIGIOUS LEADERS, AFFIRMED THAT JESUS PERFORMED DISPLAYS OF SUPERNATURAL POWER.

Doré, Gustave. *Resurrection of Lazarus.* Ca. 1875. www.wikiart.org..

5. Jesus Would Be Crucified for Our Sins In Jerusalem In the Month of Passover (Nisan) 33 A.D. That We Might Have Eternal Life

Daniel → The Messiah will come to Jerusalem during the month of Passover in 33 A.D., after which he will be put to death

We are next going to examine a powerful prophecy from the book of Daniel, chapter 9. I call this one the "smoking gun" of the Bible as it is astonishingly accurate in the timing and the details of the events it portrays. It's going to take a little math, so please bear with me.

Daniel started off this chapter by petitioning God to end Israel's seventy-year Babylonian exile as foretold by Jeremiah; God sent an angel to carry a reply. This is the first part of the angel's response:

> [24]*"Seventy 'sevens' are decreed for your people and your holy city to finish transgression, to put an end to sin, to atone for wickedness, to bring in everlasting righteousness, to seal up vision and prophecy and to anoint the Most Holy Place [or Holy One]."*
>
> [25]*"Know and understand this: From the time the word goes out to restore and rebuild <u>Jerusalem</u> until the <u>Anointed One, the ruler,</u> comes, there will be <u>seven 'sevens,'</u> and <u>sixty-two 'sevens.'</u> It will be rebuilt with streets and a trench, but in times of trouble."*
>
> [26]*"After the sixty-two 'sevens,' the Anointed One will be put to death and will have nothing."*
>
> – DANIEL 9:24-26A (EMPHASIS AND SEPARATION MINE)

- While the entire prophecy covers a period of time called "Seventy Sevens," in this chapter we are only concerned with the first half of the prophecy, which deals with only the passing of 69 of those "sevens" (7 Sevens + 62 Sevens). The meaning of the sevens is explained below.

- This prophecy breaks down into three events: (1) The decree to rebuild Jerusalem, (2) the passing of time of the 69 Sevens, and (3) the coming of the Anointed Ruler ("Messiah" in Hebrew) to Jerusalem followed by his death.

1) The decree was given by King Artaxerxes I in the second chapter of Nehemiah. Artaxerxes I was king of Persia from 465 to 425 B.C. His twentieth year began in 445 B.C., with the Jewish month of Nisan bringing the actual time of this decree to spring of 444 B.C (Britannica 2014, "Artaxerxes I"). Nehemiah was the king's Jewish cupbearer at the time in the city of Susa.

> "In the *month of Nisan* in the *twentieth year of King Artaxerxes,* when wine was brought for him, I took the wine and gave it to the king . . . He asked the king, 'If it pleases the king and if your servant has found favor in his sight, *let him send me to the city in Judah [Jerusalem]* where my ancestors are buried *so that I can rebuild it* . . . *It pleased the king to send me* . . . because the gracious hand of my God was on me, the king granted my requests [for safe passage to Judah and for building resources]."
> – NEHEMIAH 2:1, 5, 6B, 8B (EMPHASIS AND BRACKETS MINE)

And so, King Artaxerxes gave Nehemiah leave to go rebuild Jerusalem and its walls. We now have our reference start time for this prophecy: **Nisan (March/April), 444 B.C.**

2) **The 69 Sevens:** Under the Mosaic Law a "seven" was a seven-year cyclical period of debt-cancellation. Every seven years, Israelites were commanded to release each other from any debts or servitude left unpaid so as not to have a permanent institution of slavery amongst themselves (Deut. 15). We can think of it as 69 "weeks" of years.

While the original Hebrew simply means "a period of seven," we can also know that a "seven" refers to years based on the context of earlier in the chapter, where Daniel was thinking in terms of years when referencing the Babylonian captivity period of 70 years (Dan. 9:2). The angel speaking to Daniel was essentially carrying that thought from "70 years" to "70 times 7 years" in verse 24. For the first part of the prophecy, we are focusing on 69 of these sevens:

> **69 x 7 years = 483 years**

Prophetic Years: It's important to note that the prophets of the Bible operated under a 360-day lunar calendar. The 360-day calendar was originally used in ancient antiquity (in the times of Genesis); the prophets maintained this calendar throughout the Bible for continuity even though most cultures had moved on to a 365-day calendar system or a leap-month system. Revelation 11:2 gives a perfect example of this: 42 months being equivalent to 1,260 days, which breaks down evenly into 30-day months (1,260/42=30, which is what is used in a 360-day calendar).

- With this in mind, we need to convert from Prophetic years to our modern Gregorian years of 365.25 days.

483 Prophetic years x 360 days per year = 173,880 days
173,880 days / 365.25 days per Gregorian year = 476 years
69 "sevens" = 476 Gregorian Years

| Decree to rebuild Jerusalem (Nisan 444 B.C.) | → | 69 Sevens (476 Years) | → | Anointed Ruler comes to Jerusalem and is put to death |

3) Now we can figure out the predicted time of arrival for this Anointed Ruler, the Messiah, by adding the 476 years to the start reference of Nisan, 444 B.C.:

476 – 444 B.C. = Nisan, 32 A.D.
➢ Since there is no "year zero" between B.C. and A.D., we add a year to the final date
= NISAN, 33 A.D.

This is the month and year by which the Gospels *and* our historical sources date the coming of Jesus to Jerusalem and his ensuing crucifixion about a week later (see "Dating the Crucifixion" below). Both Josephus and Tacitus confirm Jesus' death under Pontius Pilate, who was governor of Judea from 26–36 A.D., and the Mishnah places his death around the time of Passover. The prophets, the Gospels, and the ancient historians all agree on the timing and circumstances of this specific event.

| Decree to rebuild Jerusalem (Nisan 444 B.C.) | → | 69 Sevens (476 Years) | → | Anointed Ruler comes to Jerusalem and is put to death (Nisan 33 A.D.) |

DANIEL PREDICTED THE COMING OF JESUS TO JERUSALEM DOWN TO THE YEAR AND MONTH! HOW AWESOME THAT HE ALSO LIKELY DIED FOR OUR SINS DURING A JEWISH YEAR OF DEBT CANCELLATION!

Again, I have to reemphasize—this prophecy was penned at least 134 years before the coming of Jesus to Jerusalem as Messiah. Even if that means it was written after Artaxerxes' decree, the chances of randomly guessing the coming of Jesus down to the month are astronomical. If this was just written by some

© Zatletic. *Palm Sunday.*
Accessed July 15, 2015. www.canstockphoto.com

religious nut, it would have just been a stab in the dark. He wouldn't have known if the Messiah was going to come in 100 years or 10,000 years. And, if Daniel really wrote this when he said he did, then this prophecy was written over 500 years before Jesus' coming and over 100 years before the decree. God's hand is all over this prophecy—it's the only way it could be so precise. As we'll see in the next chapter, the next half of this prophecy doesn't disappoint either.

King David → Painted detailed experience of a crucifixion scene

"¹⁴I am poured out like water, and all my bones are out of joint. My heart has turned to wax; it has melted within me. ¹⁵My mouth is dried up like a potsherd, and my tongue sticks to the roof of my mouth; you lay me in the dust of death. ¹⁶Dogs surround me, a pack of villains encircles me; they pierce my hands and my feet. ¹⁷All my bones are on display; people stare and gloat over me."
– Psalms 22:14-17

These verses give an accurate depiction of the physiological effects of a crucifixion (which did not exist as an execution method until seven to eight hundred years later).

There is no apparent reason for David to have written this—it does not pertain to anything we know about his life; it is widely accepted as one of his many prophetic references to the Messiah.

- Verse 14: Depicts how the effects of a crucifixion result in the pericardium sac around the heart filling up with fluid. A spear piercing the heart would cause that fluid to flow out like water (as recounted in the Gospels). This verse is also accurate in its description of the bones. Hanging for hours on a cross would slowly pull joints apart as muscles and ligaments gave out.

- Verse 15: A crucifixion victim would suffer from severe dehydration and blood loss.

- Verse 16: Both hands and feet were nailed to wood during a crucifixion. The encircling "dogs" are a direct parallel to the Romans that would perform these executions and stand guard to ensure death.

Rubens, Peter Paul. *Christ on the Cross Between Two Thieves.* 1620. Royal Museum of Fine Arts, Antwerp, Belguim. Commons.wikimedia.org.

- Verse 17: A crucifixion put the victim on humiliating naked display for all to see.

King David's Psalms seem to contain many allusions to events surrounding the coming Messiah as if experienced by David himself. The Messiah, after all, was to be a descendant of David's royal line as we've already seen in other prophecies, so in a way these events were going to happen to him.

Isaiah → The Servant would be "pierced" and killed for transgressions of God's people

"Just as there were many who were appalled at him [God's Servant]— his appearance was so disfigured beyond that of any human being and

> *his form marred beyond human likeness . . . Surely he took up our pain and bore our suffering, yet we considered him punished by God, stricken by him, and afflicted. But <u>he was pierced for our transgressions</u>, he was crushed for our iniquities; the punishment that brought us peace was upon him, and by <u>his wounds we are healed</u>. . .*
> *For <u>he was cut off from the land of the living; for the transgression of my people he was punished</u>.*"
> – ISAIAH 52:14; 53:4-5, 8B (EMPHASIS MINE)

- Again we see the imagery of the Messiah being brutally punished and specifically, "pierced." The Gospels describe that Jesus was beaten, had a crown of thorns put on his head, was severely flogged, nailed to and hung on a cross, then pierced by a spear. Again, the term "crucifixion" was not used, as it would have been unfamiliar to the Jews of the eighth century B.C. to whom this was written—this form of execution had not yet been invented.

© Bernard Dunne. *Jesus the Messiah Savior of the World.*
Accessed July 11, 2015. 123rf.com.

- The Servant was to be a sacrifice of atonement for the sins of the Jewish people (and, as we'll see, for those of the entire world)—a perfect final sacrifice under the Mosaic Covenant.

BOTH DAVID AND ISAIAH PAINT GRAPHIC IMAGES OF THE FATE OF THIS MESSIAH, JESUS. BEFORE HE WOULD ASSUME THE THRONE OF HIS KINGDOM, HE WAS TO BE CRUCIFIED AND DIE AS THE SACRAFICIAL LAMB FOR THE SINS OF THE WORLD

Dating the Crucifixion

While Josephus and Tacitus give us a window of time for the Jesus' crucifixion, we can narrow it down to the exact date and hour when cross-referencing with historical data from the Gospels. The gospel writers give us five clues, which allow us to home in on the timing of Jesus' death:

1) All four Gospels agree with Tacitus and Josephus that Jesus was crucified on the orders of Pontius Pilate (Matt. 27:24-26, Mark. 15:15, Luke 23:24, John 19:15-16). This, as previously stated, gives us a starting range of 26-36 A.D.

2) The gospel of Luke tells us that the ministry of John the Baptist began "In the fifteenth year of the reign of Tiberius Caesar . . . The word of God came to John the son of Zechariah in the wilderness" (Luke 3:1-2). Since Tiberius began his reign in 14 A.D., this brings us to around 29 A.D. All four Gospels place the time of Jesus' ministry sometime after John's began, so we now have a window between 29 and 36 A.D.

3) All four Gospels tell us that Jesus was crucified on the Day of Preparation of the Passover, which was the day before the Sabbath or Friday (Matt. 27:62, Mark 15:42, Luke 23:54, John 19:42). Now we just need to narrow down which Friday between 29 and 36 A.D.

4) Passover would have begun at sundown on Friday per Jewish practice. The only Friday start-date for the Passover between 29 and 36 A.D. was Friday, April 3, 33 A.D., which has been derived from astronomical data (http://www.judaismvschristianity.com/Passover_dates.htm).

5) The Gospels tell us that Jesus died around the ninth hour of the day (Matt. 27:45-50, Mark 15:34-37, Luke 23:44-46); by Jewish reckoning, that was 3:00 p.m.

JESUS PERISHED AROUND 3:00 P.M. ON FRIDAY, APRIL 3, 33 A.D.

All the data lines up from the prediction of Daniel to the Gospels to Josephus and Tacitus, all the way to modern astronomy! Daniel 9 is the kind of prophecy only God could deliver in all his perfect planning.

What about calendar error? If our calendar system is messed up, then the Daniel 9 prophecy goes out the window, right? Our current Christian year numbering system is based around the birth of Christ in one A.D. It was developed by a sixth-century monk named

Dionysius Exiguus, who tried to use biblical references to center the old Julian Calendar system around Jesus' birth. Both modern scholars and even the Catholic Church have determined that Dionysius was several years off in his calculations. If we corrected for this year-error, that means that Jesus didn't actually die in 33 A.D. Was all this prophecy for nothing, then? Absolutely not!

Even if we made said correction in our year system, it would have no impact on the accuracy of the Daniel 9 prophecy. It's the *time difference* between Artaxerxes' decree and the final coming of Jesus to Jerusalem that matters, not the dates themselves. If we shift the year number of Jesus' birth to the left by a few years, then we also have to shift *all* historical dates by a few years, because all other dates are based on that event. If Jesus was actually born in, say, 3 B.C., and we adjusted all historical events by an error of three years, then Artaxerxes' decree would have been made in 447 B.C. and Jesus' coming and following crucifixion would have taken place in 30 A.D. It's just shifting numbers around, while the actual number of days stays the same. The decree and Jesus' coming would still be 476 years apart.

6. Jesus Would Rise from the Dead On The Third Day after His Death

Isaiah → After the Servant's death, God will prolong his days, and he will see the fruits of his labors and be satisfied

> *"Yet it pleased the Lord to bruise Him; He has put Him to grief. When You <u>make His soul an offering for sin</u> He shall <u>see His seed</u>, He [The Lord] shall <u>prolong His days</u>, and the pleasure of the Lord shall prosper in His hand. He shall <u>see the labor of His soul</u>, and be satisfied."*
> – ISAIAH 53:10-11A (NKJV; EMPHASIS AND BRACKETS MINE)

This passage tells us that Jesus' mission of providing atonement for sin would be accomplished, and the Messiah would live again to see it. "His seed" and "the labor of His soul" refer to the believers that have come about from his sacrifice and resurrection. Indeed, today, after two millennia, we can see that millions if not billions over this time have come to believe in Jesus—the labor of his soul has been very fruitful, and he has been alive to see it all!

David → God's Holy One will not see decay but will be shown life and lifted up to the right hand of God

© Designpics. *Resurrection of Jesus*
Accessed July 11, 2015. 123rf.com

"For You will not leave my soul in Sheol [Hades],
Nor will You allow Your Holy One to see corruption.
You will show me the path of life; In Your presence is fullness of joy;
At Your right hand are pleasures forevermore ..."
– Psalms 16:10-11 (NKJV; emphasis and brackets mine)

- David might have been a chosen one, but he certainly was not a holy one. Only God is considered holy in Scripture. We can see again how David was speaking through somebody else's perspective here, namely that of the coming Messiah.

- This prophecy is saying that God would not allow the Messiah, an extension of himself, to remain dead, but that he would return him to life and ascend to God's right hand.

- This messianic prophecy was claimed by Jesus when he said, "From now on, the Son of Man will be seated at the right hand of the mighty God" (Luke 22:69).

Hosea → God will restore Israel in a matter of three days

"Come, let us [Israel] return to the Lord. He has torn us to pieces but he will heal us; he has injured us but he will bind up our wounds. After two days he will revive us; on the third day he will restore us, that we may live in his presence."
– Hosea 6:1-2 (emphasis and brackets mine)

- We know that this Scripture points to Jesus because if God was to restore Israel in such a way as to allow them to live in his presence, he would have to remove their sin. According to the Genesis 3, sin is the reason we are separated from God. As we've already seen in Isaiah 52 and 53, this restoration was to be the purpose of the Servant, Jesus, in coming to die to atone for our sin and reconnect us with God.

- Jesus' resurrection on the third day completed this idea of restoration in that Israelites (and all of us) first had to die to their sins and allow God to make them something new. Accepting his death and resurrection is part of the redemption process.

THE PROPHETS PREDICTED THAT JESUS WOULD RISE FROM THE DEAD ON THE THIRD DAY, WHICH IS EXACTLY WHAT HIS EARLY FOLLOWERS BELIEVED OF HIM.

7. Christianity Would Spread Rapidly around the World and Bring Great Moral Change to Those Who Follow It

Moses → All the nations would be blessed through the seed of Abraham

God made a promise to Abraham:

> *"I will surely bless you and make your descendants as numerous as the stars in the sky and as the sand on the seashore. Your descendants will take possession of the cities of their enemies, and through your offspring all nations on earth will be blessed, because you have obeyed me."*
> – Genesis 22:17-18 (emphasis mine)

- Abraham's physical descendants (the Jews) and spiritual descendants (all believers) past and present are indeed as numerous as the stars. Jesus, who came from Abraham's line, is known to most of the world and has brought about blessings of hope and a radical change for good. No other name is known like that of Jesus. His blessings continue to spread to this day.

Isaiah → The Servant will bring salvation to Israel and to the ends of the earth

> *"It is too small a thing for you to be my servant to restore the tribes of Jacob and bring back those of Israel I have kept. I will also make you a light for the Gentiles, that my salvation may reach to the ends of the earth."*
> – ISAIAH 49:6

- Isaiah predicted the coming of Christianity through the Messiah, which would bring salvation to the entire world, not just the Jews. Our ancient sources confirmed that this new way of belief did in fact start with the Jews and spread out to the Gentiles (non-Jews) very rapidly.

- Not only did Christianity spread like wildfire into Asia Minor and Europe in the years of the apostles, but it also exploded into Northern Africa and even made its way as far as India.

Isaiah → A new path of righteousness will originate from Israel

Isaiah prophesying about the future Israel:

> *"And a highway will be there [Israel]; it will be called the <u>Way of Holiness</u>; it will be for those who walk on that Way. The unclean will not journey on it; wicked fools will not go about on it . . . But only the redeemed will walk there, and those the Lord has rescued will return."*
> – ISAIAH 35:8-10 (EMPHASIS AND BRACKETS MINE)

- This is a continuation from the section predict-

© Kevin Carden.
Accessed July 11, 2015. 123rf.com.

ing God would come and do miracles among Israel. Isaiah was predicting the coming of a new way of morality and living after God came to save and redeem them.

- Judaism already existed well before this prophecy was written, so this could not be referring to Israel's belief system at that time—these verses are speaking of redemption to come (Christianity). In fact, before the term "Christianity" was coined, the religion was simply referred to as "The Way" in its early days (Acts 9:2, 19:23), just as it is here.

ALL THE EARTH HAS INDEED BEEN BLESSED BY JESUS, AND MANY HAVE CHOSEN TO WALK IN HIS WAY OF HOLINESS AND REDEMPTION AS THE PROPHETS FORETOLD MANY YEARS BEFORE HIS COMING.

COMBINING THE EVIDENCE

The second line of evidence is in! Not only do we have testimony from historians supporting the truth of the Gospels' seven claims, we have testimony from the prophets who foretold all these claims at least a hundred years before Jesus was even born. For the record, the prophets predicted, the gospel-writers gave witness, and non-Christian history affirms that

1. **There would be an influential man by the name of Jesus (also called Christ), who would be the Jewish King And Messiah** → Historians have proven that this man did exist, and just as the NT writers described, many came to believe Jesus was a King and Messiah during and immediately after his life on Earth.
2. **Jesus would live a wise and virtuous life** → Everything we know about Jesus through the Gospels, the apostles, and non-biblical sources affirm this was true about him. It was one of the reasons he was so influential and so well-loved.

3. **Jesus, the Messiah, would be God in the flesh** → The fact that many Jews and Gentiles came to believe and worship Jesus as God has been affirmed in the earliest accounts of Christianity all the way back to the first century. Such a rapid proliferation of this belief amongst the strictly monotheistic Jews is powerful testimony that they had strong reasons to believe it. Because of this early testimony, we can also lay to rest any theory about Jesus' deity being legend or written back into the Gospels hundreds of years after his life on Earth.

4. **Jesus would perform miracles** → Jesus' enemies confirmed in writing that he performed supernatural feats they called "sorcery." Since we've already established that Jesus was seen as virtuous, it's safe to assume he wielded this "sorcery" for good; therefore, we can call these feats "miracles."

5. **Jesus would be crucified for our sins in Jerusalem during the month of Passover (Nisan) 33 A.D. that we might have eternal life** → Roman, Greek, and Jewish historians confirm that Jesus was indeed crucified on the eve of a Passover under Pontius Pilate, who ruled Judea from 26 to 36 A.D. Cross-referencing historical references in the Gospels and secular history reveals that this Friday Passover could only have occurred in 33 A.D. First century Christians believed that Jesus died as atonement for sins in order to remove the curse of spiritual death and bring us eternal life.

6. **Jesus would rise from the dead on the third day after his death** → Jesus' followers did, in fact, believe very early on that he rose from the dead on the third day after his crucifixion. It was the major reason for their belief that he was God and Messiah.

7. **Christianity would spread rapidly around the world and bring great moral change to those who follow it** → Our historians affirm that Christianity did spread very rapidly around the world soon after 33 A.D. and brought great moral and spiritual change to those who followed it.

One cannot underestimate the significance of all these things being specifically predicted hundreds of years before they took place. One or two prophecies coming together, maybe, but the odds of even the fourteen mentioned here coming together around one man at the right time and place would be astronomical. God's hand is all over this—it's just too convenient to be lucky guesswork.

Let's look at it this way: Could the prophets have just randomly guessed that there would be a man named Joshua (Jesus' Hebrew name) who was to die in 33 A.D? Sure—I could predict that a man named Bob will die twenty years from now and probably get it right. But what these prophets did was so much more. They predicted that a man named Joshua would come and lead a sinless life; perform miracles for Israel; have such influence as to be considered the Jewish king, Messiah, and God; that he would be crucified in Jerusalem in the month of Nisan, 33 A.D. for the sins of the world; then would rise again three days later and thereafter witness the spreading of his gospel around the world. These prophets knew exactly whom they were talking about! (I'd like to point out, too, that there are over a hundred prophecies in the OT that give us even more clarity on Jesus as the Messiah—I've only focused on those prophecies which are verified as fulfilled through non-Christian sources for the sake of skepticism.)

What we are beholding, here, is something supernatural in these prophets predicting such details about one man. If they had access to the supernatural, is it that much more of a stretch to believe supernatural things about Jesus?

And since we have early corroboration from non-Christian sources on all the above facts and beliefs, we know that the gospel writers did not just fabricate Jesus' fulfillment of all these prophecies—Jesus lived them out and people believed it! What, then, are the implications?

Conclusions about the Messiah

1. **Jesus perfectly embodied the figure predicted by all these prophecies and attested to by history—they all work together to point to him alone.**

➢ There are no others before or since who could meet the prophetic criteria for Messiah. We have specific events and dates that have already come to pass. The powerful effect of Jesus' coming can be seen even today, over two thousand years later. What more proof is necessary that he was/is the prophesied Messiah?

2. No mere man could have manipulated all of these characteristics and events to come true in himself.

➢ Based on prophecies and historical reports, we are left with two options: Either Jesus was God and fulfilled all the dozens of messianic prophecies according to his plan or we are to believe that a crazy, poor carpenter carefully studied all the messianic prophecies and was able to manipulate his life and that of hundreds of others to flawlessly bring about the fulfillment of every single prophecy at just the right time in history. Along the way he fooled many into thinking he was God by somehow healing hundreds, casting out demons, raising the dead, and faking his own death and resurrection. It would be a conspiracy of epic proportions! Which is more rational and easier to believe given the evidence?

3. Jesus was God and Messiah, born as a man to be the sinless substitute for the punishment due to mankind.

➢ We have historical proof that the idea of Jesus' divinity and resurrection wasn't invented hundreds of years later but was already in place within one to two generations of his life. Hardly enough time for a myth to take root from a few writers' crazy stories. People claimed to have seen his divine miracles and his post-resurrection appearances firsthand— why would they have gone to their deaths claiming this if they knew it was a lie?

➢ Whether we want to admit it or not, we are ALL sinners in need of a savior. We can never achieve perfection on our own to win the favor of a perfect, holy God. "For all have

sinned and fall short of the glory of God, and all are justified freely by his grace through the redemption that came by
Christ Jesus" (Rom. 3:23-24).

**4. Jesus taught that the only way to salvation was belief and trust
in him alone.**

> ➤ If Jesus really was God and therefore all he teaches is true,
> then this is the final conclusion. We can choose Jesus or not,
> but there are no alternatives—he didn't leave room for any:
>
> - "I am the Way and the truth and the life. No one
>   comes to the Father except through me" (John 14:6).
>
> - "Whoever acknowledges me before others, I will
>   also acknowledge before my Father in heaven. But
>   whoever disowns me before others, I will disown
>   before my Father in heaven" (Matt. 10:32-33).
>
> - "For the wages of sin is death, but the gift of God is
>   eternal life in Christ Jesus our Lord" (Rom. 6:23).
>
> - "For God so loved the world that He gave His only
>   begotten Son, that whoever believes in him should
>   not perish but have everlasting life" (John 3:16).
>
> - "Salvation is found in no one else, for there is no oth-
>   er name under heaven given to mankind by which
>   we must be saved" (Acts 4:12).

These are serious implications for all our lives if what Jesus and
his apostles said is true. In light of all the evidence we've examined, is
it so hard to believe that the Gospels got it right with these claims as
well? Thousands upon thousands of people in the early first century
had good reason for believing so. What are you willing to accept about
this man named Jesus? The evidence is in, but only you can decide the
verdict for yourself. He's standing at your door and knocking right
now . . . will you let him in as your Lord and Savior?

I'm Still Skeptical

So, Jesus was real, he really was crucified, and there's no doubt about the impact he had on the world in the short time thereafter. But couldn't the apostles have somehow just made Jesus into this divine messiah figure by fooling people that he rose from the dead and by saying that the he fulfilled all the OT prophecies? They had a religious agenda to push! If you are still suspicious of apostolic shenanigans, then I want to make sure we leave no stone unturned.

We can know for sure that the apostles did not fabricate their claims about Jesus as God and Messiah. Such an act is something they simply would not have done, nor could they have given the circumstances. First of all, the messiah they described was not the messiah that the Jews were expecting or wanted. They were expecting the prophesied Messiah to immediately triumph over Israel's oppressors and take the throne of David. "A Messiah who failed to deliver and to reign, who was defeated, humiliated, and slain by his enemies, is a contradiction in terms" (Craig 2008, 388). This is not the type of messiah the disciples would invent if they wanted the Jews to buy into a lie. They would have been humiliated and devastated by Jesus' death and would have looked for their messiah elsewhere, not try to turn him into a deity by saying he rose from the dead (Craig 2008, 372).

Further complicating the idea of such a hoax is that the Jews had no concept of a temporal resurrection of one individual. Their only concept of resurrection was that of the End Times, when God would come to judge the world and establish his kingdom (Craig 2008, 392-393). Martha, a disciple of Jesus, voiced this concept in John 11:23-24. A made-up story about Jesus' resurrection would have been rejected by the Jews on both these prior counts if there wasn't strong evidence to support it.

More importantly, a hoaxed resurrection cannot explain the sudden changes in the apostles' religious beliefs and willingness to suffer and die for the sake of propagating them. They would have been claiming witness to a resurrection they never saw, having seen Jesus' death on the cross, and would therefore have been using known lies to teach his virtues. They would have gone against the well-established Jewish and Roman religions, all the while knowing they would bring upon themselves persecution and death for no rational reason (Paley 1796, 1:327-328). Only a life-changing event such as the resurrection would have generated this extreme behavior.

And even if they had wanted to fake Jesus' resurrection or had perhaps somehow been fooled, it would have been impossible to start up a religion around this event in Jerusalem—the very city in which Jesus' trial and execution took place—unless there was solid evidence for the resurrection having occurred. Hundreds of thousands of people were in the city for Passover and would have witnessed or at least heard of the events of Jesus' last day—he was paraded with a cross through the city streets! It would take some significant evidence to convince the masses that Jesus rose from the dead after his very public execution. It would be akin to someone trying to prove the 9/11 attacks never happened—millions saw the planes hit the Twin Towers and their following collapse into rubble. To convince someone otherwise would require the towers to be standing and the people who died shown to be alive. Jesus' resurrection and bodily appearances to hundreds thereafter present the only plausible explanation for the rise of the Christian church in Jerusalem.

Either way we look at it, skeptics still have to be able to explain away the amazingly specific prophecies about Jesus, which have been verified as fulfilled by even non-Christian sources. One cannot deny that something much more than really lucky guesswork is going on here.

Still unconvinced that these prophets could tell the future and that the Bible is the true Word of God? Hold on . . . there's more to come!

ROME: GOD'S CURSE FULFILLED

"For these are the days of vengeance, that all things which are written may be fulfilled. For there will be great distress in the land and wrath upon this people. And they will fall by the edge of the sword, and be led away captive into all nations. And Jerusalem will be trampled by Gentiles until the times of the Gentiles are fulfilled."
—LUKE 21:22, 23B-24

The year is 66 A.D. It has been thirty-three years since the resurrection and ascension of Jesus. Christianity has exploded out of Jerusalem into all parts of the Roman Empire—carried forward by the motivated feet and preaching of Jesus' many disciples. Believers everywhere are falling under the persecution of the Roman emperor, Nero, who blamed them for the burning of Rome. Paul, the first apostle to the Gentiles, is on his way to Rome to face his own fate for preaching the gospel.

Back in Palestine, tensions are growing between the Romans and the Jews. Gessius Florus, the new Roman procurator of Judea, has been inciting the Jews to revolt through religious harassment. After provoking protests by stealing money from the temple's treasury, he retaliates by allowing his soldiers to plunder parts of Jerusalem, during which several thousand Jews are mindlessly slaughtered and some crucified. The downward spiral of chaos begins, Jewish factions begin to form and compete for power, and it isn't long before a Roman

Legion is brought into Judea to quell the uprising. Surprisingly, the Jewish rebels prevail against the Romans in battle at Beth Horon, massacring around six thousand troops. The war is on! Emperor Nero, recognizing the seriousness of the situation, knows that he needs someone experienced to take care of business—enter General Vespasian.

What followed was the great tribulation of Israel's time, predicted both by Jesus (see above) and by the prophets of the Old Testament. It was Moses who first warned those early Israelites of this calamity should they fail to uphold their covenant with God in the land he was about to give them. In spite of reminders from other prophets over the centuries, that warning went unheeded, to the ruin of their entire civilization. What we are about to uncover is how this devastating event was foretold by the prophets and fulfilled in history years later.

HISTORY OF THE FIRST AND SECOND JEWISH-ROMAN WARS

Once again, we need to have a grasp of the historical context around this next set of prophecies before we can fully understand and appreciate them. Here we pick up our timeline where we last left off with Jesus and follow it through this pivotal time period in Jewish history. Unless otherwise noted, much of the following history comes from the Jewish historian Josephus in his book *War of the Jews*.

History of Israel

33 A.D.
Resurrection and Ascension of Jesus

February 67 A.D.

Enter Vespasian. Roman general Vespasian arrives in Palestine and takes command of a multinational force of over sixty thousand troops.

May–July 67 A.D.

Vespasian enters Galilee and sieges the garrison city of Jotapata, which is under command of Josephus. The city falls along with several others. Josephus is captured and bears witness to the war thereafter.

Sep. 67–May 69 A.D.

The Romans conquer much of northern Palestine.

June–July 69 A.D.

Vespasian invades Judea. After Nero's death, he is soon proclaimed emperor and departs for Rome, leaving his army under command of his son, Titus.

April–September 70 A.D.

Titus, Vespasian's son, lays siege to the city of Jerusalem. Being the time of the feast of Passover, an estimated 1.5 to 2 million Jews are trapped inside the city walls. Famine, disease, and great slaughter ensue. Titus fights the resistance to the very walls of the temple grounds. The temple is burned, and eventually the city is demolished. Over one million are dead; thousands more are taken as captives or sold as slaves.

March 74 A.D.

Masada falls. The last of the Jewish resistance holds out at the mountain fortress of Masada. The Tenth Roman Legion lays siege to the city and builds a massive earthen ramp to bring siege works to the city's walls. Before the Romans can breach the walls, most of the inhabitants commit suicide rather than fall into Roman hands.

History of Israel

132–136 A.D.

The Second Jewish Revolt

Also known as the Bar Kokhba Revolt, this second war with the Romans was led by Simon Bar Kokhba, during the reign of Roman Emperor Hadrian, in response to plowing up the Temple Mount or possibly building a temple to Jupiter there. Simon, thought by some Jews to have been the Messiah, failed to throw off Roman oppression and, in fact, made it worse for a time. He was killed and Rome purged Judea of its Jews. Over one thousand Jewish cities were laid waste and hundreds of thousands of Jews killed. On the rubble of Jerusalem, Rome built the city of Aelia Capitolina, banning the entry of Jews or practice of their religion in an attempt to stamp out the rebellious culture (Cassius Dio, *H.R.*).

Between these two wars, the once glorious nation of Israel was laid to utter ruin and its relatively few remaining people were flung to the far reaches of the earth through sale into slavery or from fleeing the Romans. Take special note that from the coming of Vespasian during the first war to the end of the Great Revolt at Masada was seven years, almost exactly. This will be a key point for one of the prophecies to come.

Now that we have established the "big picture" of this period in Jewish history, we turn once more to the prophets of the OT. The events described above should have come as no surprise to the Jews—they were warned of the coming of Rome many centuries before. But, again, even if we only date the prophets' writings to 100 B.C., there are some startling prophecies that lay out the details of what was to become of Israel in the two centuries thereafter.

THE CURSE OF THE MOSAIC COVENANT

After the Exodus from Egypt, as the young, nomadic nation of Israel was preparing to enter the Promised Land of Canaan for the first time, Moses gathered them together to remind them of the covenant they had made with God forty years earlier at the foot of Mt. Sinai. Like several times before, he relayed God's desire to bless them in the land they were about to inherit should they keep all of God's covenantal commands. Should they fail to do so, however, Moses promised curses upon Israel of the nastiest kinds one can imagine. But this time, he mentioned a very specific curse in the form of a singular nation that would fall upon Israel in the years to come:

> *"The Lord will bring a nation against you from far away, from the ends of the earth, <u>like an eagle swooping down, a nation whose language you will not understand,</u> a fierce-looking nation without respect for the old or pity for the young . . . They will <u>lay siege to all the cities throughout your land</u> until the high fortified walls in which you trust fall down. They will besiege all the cities throughout the land the Lord your God is giving you . . . You who were as numerous as the stars in the sky will be left but few in number, because you did not obey the Lord your God . . . <u>Then the Lord will scatter you among all nations, from one end of the earth to the other. There you will worship other gods—gods of wood and stone, which neither you nor your ancestors have known.</u> Among those nations you will find no repose, no resting place for the sole of your foot. There the Lord will give you an anxious mind, eyes weary with longing, and a despairing heart . . . The <u>Lord will send you back in ships to Egypt</u> on a journey I said you should never make again.*
> *There <u>you will offer yourselves for sale to your enemies as male and female slaves, but no one will buy you.</u>"*
> –DEUTERONOMY 28: 49-50, 52, 62, 64-65, 68 (EMPHASIS MINE)

While the omitted portions of this section do describe events particular to this conflict, they are also common occurrences in any great siege of the ancient world. As we'll see shortly, however, these specific verses set this coming nation apart from all other possibilities in the history of Israel's existence. There are several historical crosshairs in the above verses that will allow us to home in on the target nation of this prophecy.

We know that the nation of ancient Israel was heavily assaulted only three times in history to the point of utter destruction: First, by <u>Assyria</u>, which conquered the northern kingdom of Israel; second, by

<u>Babylon</u>, which conquered the southern kingdom of Judah and destroyed Jerusalem and the First Temple; lastly, after Persia and Greece had peacefully annexed Israel, <u>Rome</u> ultimately wiped the entire country off the map, purging it of almost all Jews and renaming it Palestine. Our options must come from these three nations.

These remaining clues will provide us with the answer:

| **Nation from far away**
 Unfamiliar language
 Unfamiliar gods | • Israel was longtime neighbors with Assyria and Babylon; they were familiar with their languages and gods.
 • Only Rome meets these three critereon. |

| **Swoop down upon Israel like an eagle** | • The eagle was the primary battle standard of the Roman Legions and was a symbol of power for the Empire. |

| **All Israeli cities beseiged** | • Of these three nations, Rome was the only one to literally demolish all the cities of Israel. |

| **Israel scattered to the far reaches of the earth** | • The Assyrian and Babylonian empires were big and did disperse Jews throughout their land, but only Rome controlled so much territory as to have truly scattered the Jews around the world after conquering them. |

| **Israelites shipped as slaves back to Egypt** | • Assyria and Babylon were constantly at war with Egypt but never conquered it; they would not have sold slaves to their enemy.
 • Of these three, only Rome ever held control over Egypt and did in fact ship Jewish captives there to be sold as slaves. |

The first two sets of clues are a given in well-known history, but we'll see, as we explore the prophecies and history chronologically, the last three clues are confirmed by historians Flavius Josephus and Cassius Dio. Josephus, especially, will be critical in confirming the fulfillment of this and other prophecies as well.

Dating Deuteronomy 28

If Moses really wrote the first five books of the Bible (known as the Law) as biblical scholars suspect, then he knew about the coming of Rome about 650 years before Rome was even founded. But, if we're taking the skeptical approach, we know that the books of The Law were written by at least around 250 B.C., when the Hellenic King Ptolemy II had them translated into Greek for the great library in Alexandria. By that time, Rome was still far away across the Mediterranean and wasn't even a concern for Israel for another 200 years.

No matter how we look at it, the writer of Deuteronomy knew the Romans were coming well before they were a threat to Israel. And he knew that Rome was going to be the ultimate fulfillment of God's curse upon Israel for breaking their covenant with him. Moses, however, wasn't the only prophet with divine insight into the coming of Rome . . .

THE KINGDOM OF IRON

Fast-forward about eight hundred years to the prophet Daniel, who was a young servant in the courts of Babylon after they subjugated Judah and carried off many of Jerusalem's finest into captivity. Nebuchadnezzar was in the second year of his reign (603 B.C.), and had a vivid dream which he wanted the wise men of his courts to interpret for him. When the other wise men failed, Daniel stepped forward to bring glory to God by first telling the king his own dream and then interpreting it for him. This was the interpretation of that dream:

Daniel to Nebuchadnezzar:

"This was the dream, and now we will interpret it to the king. Your Majesty, you are the king of kings. The God of heaven has given you dominion and power and might and glory . . . After you, another kingdom will arise, inferior to yours. Next, a third kingdom, one of bronze, will rule over the whole earth. Finally, there will be a fourth kingdom, strong as iron—for iron breaks and smashes everything—and as iron breaks things to pieces, so it will crush and break all the others."
–DANIEL 2:36-37, 39-40

Here, Daniel foretold the rise and fall of kingdoms to come. He predicted that Babylon would lose its kingdom to another, which it did in 539 B.C. when the Medo-Persian Empire conquered Babylon and claimed their territory for their own. (Van De Mieroop 2007, 287). Next, a "kingdom of bronze" would supplant Persia as the world power. Greece, known for its success in combat due to use of bronze armor, swept over the Persian Empire and conquered it in 331 B.C. (Van De Mieroop 2007, 300). Finally a "kingdom, strong as iron" was to come in and destroy the Greek Empire. Rome is historically recognized by its advances in the technology of iron and its widespread use in the military to dominate all nations before it. Rome conquered the Greek peninsula in 146 B.C. (Worldmark 2007, s.v. "Greece") and finished conquering the divided kingdoms of the old Greek Empire by 30 B.C. with the defeat of the Ptolemaic Kingdom.

© Standby. *Into the Heat of Battle.* 2007. Istockphoto.com.

Indeed, world events happened just as Daniel predicted. Rome did eventually take control of Israel and effectively conquered all the kingdoms that had once ruled over them. Rome then subjugated Israel in 63 B.C. If this prophecy was given in 603 B.C. like the writer claims, then Daniel, like Moses, foresaw the coming of Rome to Israel over five centuries before it happened. At that time, Rome was barely on the scene of history in far-away Italy. Even if we can only date Daniel to 100 B.C., the writer still displayed foresight in predicting that Rome would conquer all of Greece's former empire by 70 years later, culminating with the fall of Egypt.

Both Moses and Daniel warned of Rome's coming—indeed the Kingdom of Iron from far away swooped down upon Israel in 63 B.C., catching them off guard and ending their century of independence. It wasn't until 130 years later that this prophesied nation of judgment would begin to fulfill God's curse upon Israel.

THE "70TH SEVEN"

Besides alluding to the coming of Rome, the prophet Daniel revealed additional details about what they would do to tiny Israel. We return to the book of Daniel chapter 9 to the second half of Gabriel's prophetic message. Following the messianic prophecy of the 69 sevens discussed last chapter, Gabriel revealed to Daniel the events of the final seven years or the "70th seven," which was to come after the death of the Messiah.

Sometime after the death of the Messiah:

> *"The people of the ruler who will come will destroy the city and the sanctuary. The end will come like a flood: War will continue until the end, and desolations have been decreed. He will confirm a covenant with many for one 'seven.' In the middle of the 'seven' he will put an end to sacrifice and offering. And at the temple he will set up an abomination that causes desolation, until the end that is decreed is poured out on him."*
> *–DANIEL 9:26B-27*

In two short verses, Daniel described some of the major details of this final seven-year period of destruction and judgment upon Israel, to which Jesus himself made reference in the Gospels. As we relate parts of this prophecy to the historical events to come, we will see that this prophecy can only relate to the Great Revolt, which led to the destruction of Jerusalem and its temple in 70 A.D.

As we've learned, the only other kingdom to utterly destroy Jerusalem and the temple was Babylon, but we know this prophecy cannot refer to them, because it is speaking of events to take place after the coming of the Messiah, Jesus. As we have learned, Jesus lived hundreds of years after Babylon fell to Persia.

Now that we're familiar with these three prophecies, I will break them down and show how they were fulfilled in history one event at a time.

THE GREAT TRIBULATION OF ISRAEL

"For then there will be great distress, unequaled from the beginning of the world until now—and never to be equaled again" (Matt. 24:21). Words echoed by Josephus in the preface to his book *The War of the Jews*: "Whereas the war which the Jews made with the Romans hath been the greatest of all those, not only that have been in our times, but, in a manner, of those that ever were heard of." It was an event not only foreseen by Jesus, but also by the prophets, hundreds if not thousands of years beforehand.

While time and space does not permit me to go into the war in great detail, I will focus on those key aspects of the war that were foretold by the prophets. Now that I have summarized the major prophecies relating to these events, I will endeavor to show chronologically how they came to fulfillment in history.

Moses and Daniel → Rome will come to destroy Israel

"The Lord will bring a nation against you from far away, from the ends of the earth, like an eagle swooping down . . ."
–Deuteronomy 28:49- 67

→

Josephus providing an overview of his book The War of the Jews:
"I shall relate . . . how the war broke out in the <u>twelfth year of Nero</u> . . . and what places the Jews assaulted in a hostile manner in the first sallies of the war . . . and how . . . Vespasian, with the elder of his sons made an expedition into the country of Judea."
–Josephus, W.J. Preface, para. 7 and 8 (emphasis mine)

"Finally, there will be a fourth kingdom, strong as iron . . . as iron breaks things to pieces, so it will crush and break all the others [other kingdoms]."
–Daniel 2:40

→

Twelfth Year of Nero = 66 A.D.

© cjh145200. Bust of Emperor Nero. 2009. Musei Capitolini, Rome. Commons.wikimedia.org.

Here we have testimony that Rome did in fact engage in a war with Israel. The chaos that led up to the full invasion by Rome started in 66 A.D. Moses predicted the coming of this faraway nation as the culmination of God's curse upon Israel for the breaking of their covenant with him. This kingdom, bearing the symbol of the eagle and empowered by iron to conquer the nations, did indeed swoop down upon Israel.

Daniel → The commander of the Roman army will make a covenant with many for seven years against the Jews

"He [the ruler to come] will confirm a covenant with many for one 'seven.'"
–DANIEL 9:27A
(BRACKETS MINE)

→

"And as he [Nero] was deliberating . . . who might be best able to punish the Jews for their rebellion . . . he found no one but <u>Vespasian</u> equal to the task, and able to undergo the great burden of so mighty a war . . . he sent this man to take command of the armies that were in Syria."
–JOSEPHUS, W.J., 3.1.2, 3.1.3 (EMPHASIS AND BRACKETS MINE)

© Shakko. Bust of Emperor Vespasian. 2007. Pushkin Museum, Moscow. En.wikipedia.org

"Vespasian sent his son Titus . . . to Alexandria, to bring back with him the 5th and 10th legions, while he himself . . . came by land into Syria, where he gathered together the Roman forces with a considerable number of auxiliaries from kings in that neighborhood . . . kings Antiochus, and Agrippa, and Sohemus . . . Malchus also, the king of Arabia . . . <u>when all were united together,</u> amounted to sixty thousand . . ."
–JOSEPHUS, W.J., 3.1.3, 3.4.2 (EMPHASIS AND BRACKETS MINE)

General Vespasian, the Roman-emperor-to-be, came into command of these forces around February of 67 A.D., when he arrived in Syria (Bunson 2002, 574). He assembled this army of Legions and local forces under one banner, in effect making a "covenant" or "alliance" with them against the Jews. It just so happens that this alliance of forces fought against the Jews for seven years, ending with the fall of

Masada in March of 74 A.D. (Cotton 1989, 157; Josephus, *W.J.*, 7.9.1).

February 67 A.D. – March 74 A.D. = 7 Years

We know that Vespasian is this "ruler" and the seven-year period is this war because Daniel earlier mentioned that the people of this ruler would come and destroy Jerusalem and the sanctuary (Dan. 9:26). We will see that this can only refer to the Roman siege of Jerusalem.

THE ROMANS CAME AND UNITED FORCES
AGAINST THE JEWS FOR SEVEN YEARS, AS MOSES
AND DANIEL PREDICTED.

Moses→This nation from far away will have no respect for the old or pity for the young

"The Lord will bring a nation against you from far away, from the ends of the earth, like an eagle swooping down, a nation whose language you will not understand, a fierce-looking nation without respect for the old or pity for the young . . ."
–DEUTERONOMY 28:49-50 (EMPHASIS MINE)

→

"So Vespasian marched to the city Gadara, and took it upon the first onset, because he found it destitute of any considerable number of men grown up and fit for war. He came then into it, and slew all the youth, the Romans having no mercy on any age whatsoever; and this was done out of the hatred they bore the nation . . ."
–JOSEPHUS, *W.J.*, 3.7.1

"While the holy house was on fire, every thing was plundered that came to hand, and ten thousand of those that were caught were slain; nor was there a commiseration of any age, or any reverence of gravity, but children, and old men, and profane persons, and priests were all slain in the same manner."
–JOSEPHUS, *W.J.*, 6.5.1

The Romans live up to this prophecy early in their campaign against the Jews. The Romans took out their rage on Gadara and proceeded to slaughter all its inhabitants. They then burned the city, and did the same to the towns and villages all around it, killing and taking captives for slaves as they went. This set the tone for the rest of the war.

Later, during the siege of Jerusalem, we witness this same barbarism against the young and old, who were running in fear of their lives.

Daniel→Rome will come to Jerusalem

Fast forward to 70 A.D. Vespasian has effectively conquered Galilee and has been working on his campaign in Judea. Just as he turns his sights on Jerusalem, he is called away to Rome to assume the throne as emperor. He leaves the task of finishing the war to his eldest son, Titus (who later becomes emperor after his father). And so, he brings the forces of Rome to the Jewish capital city of Jerusalem.

"From the time the word goes out to restore and rebuild Jerusalem until the Anointed One, the ruler, comes, there will be seven 'sevens,' and sixty-two 'sevens' . . . The people of the ruler who will come will destroy the city and the sanctuary."
–DANIEL 9:25-26

→

". . . he [Titus] pitched his camp at . . . 'the Valley of Thorns,' . . . being distant from Jerusalem about thirty furlongs."
–JOSEPHUS, *W.J.*, 5.2.1
(BRACKETS MINE)

"These legions [the Tenth Legion] had orders to encamp at the distance of six furlongs from Jerusalem, at the mount called the Mount of Olives which lies over against the city on the east side . . ."
–JOSEPHUS, *W.J.*, 5.2.3
(BRACKETS MINE)

Roberts, David. *The Siege and Destruction of Jerusalem.* 1850. www.preteristarchive.com.

"The city" in Daniel 9:26 is clearly a reference to Jerusalem from verse 25. So here we have Daniel predicting that this great destruction would fall upon Jerusalem.

In the spring of 70 A.D., Titus and his legions (the people of the ruler, Vespasian) lay siege to this great city, beginning the fulfillment of this prophecy.

Daniel→In the middle of the war, sacrifices at the temple will cease

Several months have passed since the beginning of the siege—it is now July, 70 A.D. Titus has pushed his way into the inner city of Jerusalem, threatening the walled grounds of the temple itself. It is here that the next portion of Daniel's prophecy became reality.

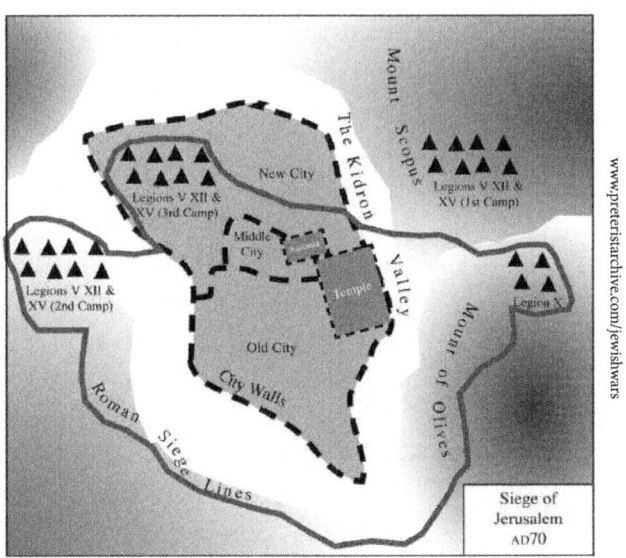

Figure 3.1 Here we see the layout of Jerusalem after the Romans had invaded the northern section of the city. Titus' next major obstacle was the stronghold fortress of Antonia and the adjoining temple grounds, which were heavily walled as well.

"*The people of the ruler who will come will destroy the city and the sanctuary . . . In the middle of the Seven he will put an end to sacrifice and offering.*"
−DANIEL 9:26B, 27B
(EMPHASIS MINE)

→

"*And now Titus gave orders to his soldiers . . . to dig up the foundations of the tower of Antonia, and make him a ready passage for his army to come up [to the temple]; for he had been informed that on that very day, which was the seventeenth day of Panemus, the sacrifice called the 'Daily Sacrifice' had failed, and had not been offered to God, for want of men to offer it . . . the people were grievously troubled at it.*"
−JOSEPHUS, *W.J.*, 6.2.1
(EMPHASIS AND BRACKETS MINE)

The "he" in Daniel 9:27 points back to "the ruler" in verse 26 who made the seven-year covenant (Vespasian). While it was Titus who physically disrupted the temple sacrifices via siege, he was still under direct authority of Emperor Vespasian, so this event is still attributed to him.

**Temple Sacrifices Ended
14 July, 70 A.D.
(17th Day of Panemus)**

Photo by Ariely. Model of Fortress of Antonia. 2008. Jerusalem. Commons.wikimedia.org.

**February, 67 A.D. → 14 July, 70 A.D. →
31 March, 74 A.D = 3.5-year point**

ROME DID IN FACT COME TO JERUSALEM, AND AT THE
MIDPOINT OF THE SEVEN-YEAR WAR WITH ROME,
SACRIFICES CAME TO AN END AT THE HOLY TEMPLE OF
GOD DUE TO THE MAYHEM OF THE ROMAN SIEGE.

Daniel → After sacrifices have ended, an abomination will be set up at the temple

Less than a month later, the Romans have finally broken through into the temple grounds, where they slaughter thousands and set fire to the Holy Temple of God. They plunder many treasures of the temple, and as they prepare to pursue the conflict into the

Unknown artist. Accessed October 24, 2014.
www.preteristarchive.com/jewishwars..

remaining parts of the city, Titus decides to stop and celebrate his progress. Daniel captured this moment in prophecy as well.

"In the middle of the Seven he will put an end to sacrifice and offering. <u>And at the temple he will set up an abomination that causes desolation, until the end that is decreed is poured out on him [or it or the city]</u>." –DANIEL 9:27 (EMPHASIS AND BRACKETS MINE)	*"And now the Romans . . . upon the burning of the holy house itself, and of all the buildings round about it, brought their ensigns to the temple and set them over against its eastern gate; and there did they offer sacrifices to them . . ."* –JOSEPHUS, W.J., 6.6.1

This last part of verse 27 is difficult to literally translate from the Hebrew into English, but the Hebrew is clear that after the temple sacrifices ceased, abominations would ensue. This act by Titus would have been an abomination of the worst kind to the Jews—sacrificing to heathen gods on the sacred grounds of the Temple of Yahweh.

AS DANIEL FORETOLD, THE ROMANS COMMITTED ABOMINATIONS ON THE TEMPLE GROUNDS AFTER THE DAILY SACRIFICE CAME TO AN END.

Daniel → Jerusalem and the temple would be destroyed

The Holy Temple has been torched and its grounds desecrated by Titus and his soldiers, as well by the blood of thousands of dead Jews. The Romans then pursue the remaining Jews into the fortified section of the upper city and even into the tunnels below it, rooting out every last man,

Unknown artist. Fall of Jerusalem. Accessed October 24, 2014. www.preteristarchive.com/ jewishwars.

woman, and child, killing and capturing many. Once this was done, the Romans put a final end to the city out of spite.

"The people of the ruler who will come will destroy the city and the sanctuary. The end will come like a flood."
–DANIEL 9:26

"And now the Romans set fire to the extreme parts of the city, and burnt them down, and entirely demolished the walls."
–JOSEPHUS, W.J., 6.9.4

"Caesar gave orders that they should now demolish the entire city and temple . . ." [Except the greatest towers and the Western Wall]
–JOSEPHUS, W.J., 6.9.4

Daniel's prophecy of this Great Tribulation comes to a climax in the events surrounding the siege and destruction of Jerusalem and the temple. Just as he predicted, the people of this "ruler to come" razed the entire city and brought great judgment upon its people as part of this final seven-year peri-od. "And thus was Jerusalem taken, in the second year of the reign of Vespasian on the eighth day of the month Gorpeius . . . [8 September, 70 A.D]" (Josephus, *W.J.* 6.10.1).

Hayez, Francisco. *The Destruction of the Jewish Temple*. 1864. En.wikipedia.org.

This final "seven" continued for another three and a half years until the last remnants of resistance were defeated at the great mountain fortress of Masada in the spring of 74 A.D. We now turn back to Moses' prophecies about the coming of Rome to see the predicted conclusions of this great curse of judgment which God put upon Israel.

Doesn't This Final Seven Reference the "End-Times" Tribulation?

The more popular/most common modern interpretation of Daniel's 70th Seven is that it describes the final seven-year period of tribulation on Earth under the Antichrist (the Beast) before Jesus' second coming. This interpretation stems from the latter half of verse 26 through verse 27:

> "The end will come like a flood: War will continue until the end, and desolations have been decreed. He [the ruler of the people that destroy the city and sanctuary] will confirm a covenant with many for one 'seven.' In the middle of the 'seven' he will put an end to sacrifice and offering. And at the temple he will set up an abomination that causes desolation, until the end that is decreed is poured out on him" (NIV; brackets mine).

These verses are often tied into the myriad of other references to a tribulation at the end of days and to the Beast referenced elsewhere in Daniel and in Revelation. There are many reasons for this interpretation, (discussion of which could amount to a book in and of itself), but I will focus on reasons why this is probably not the right interpretation of this last Seven of Daniel's 70 Sevens.

1. First, and most obviously, is that we've seen how all aspects of these verses were fulfilled in a very specific way by the events of the First Jewish-Roman War: The ruler of the Romans made an alliance with many regional rulers against Israel, which lasted seven years; without question, they were the ones

who destroyed "the city [Jerusalem] and the sanctuary"; the daily sacrifice was ended at the middle point of the seven years; and finally, abominations were committed at the temple by the son of this ruler. This is the simplest interpretation—we do not need to read more meaning into the text than this.

2. There is no other reference in the Bible to the final tribulation lasting seven years, while there are numerous references stating that it will last three and a half years. These are not the same events.

3. The "Beast" of Revelation is only given power and authority for 42 months or 3.5 years (Rev. 13:5). While the above verses do make reference to a 3.5 year milestone "in the middle of the Seven," the ruler described in Daniel 9 had power and authority for at least seven years because he established a "covenant with many" for that amount of time. 3.5 years of authority does not equal 7 years of authority, therefore, this ruler in Daniel 9 is not the Beast of the final tribulation (more on this in chapter 5).

4. "The end will come like a flood" does not necessarily refer to the end of the world. In context with the first part of verse 26, it can easily point to the end of Jerusalem and the sanctuary (which is certainly the end of the Jewish world) or the end of the Second Temple age. "War will continue to the end" can also refer back to the same event.

5. It is a huge jump in continuity to go from the end of the 69 Sevens, which was the times of Jesus, to the destruction of Jerusalem (not long after the time of Jesus), then on to the 70th Seven which will allegedly take place thousands of years later. This huge gap in time is not justified anywhere in the context of this verse—it simply does not make sense.

6. Jesus actually tells us directly what event Daniel was referring to. In Matthew 24, Jesus was speaking to his disciples about both the coming destruction of the temple and the End Times. At one point, Jesus says:

> "So when you see standing in the holy place 'the abomination that causes desolation,' spoken of through the prophet Daniel—let the reader understand— then let those who are in Judea flee to the mountains. . ." (v. 15-16).

Many draw connections to this "abomination" as the Beast of Revelation, otherwise known through Paul's writings as the "Man of Lawlessness," who will set himself up as God in the temple (2 Thess. 2:4). However, no other prophet or apostle ever refers to this man as "the abomination that causes desolation." Luke's gospel gives us more insight into Jesus' meaning during this same discourse:

> "When you see Jerusalem being surrounded by armies, you will know that its desolation is near. Then let those who are in Judea flee to the mountains, let those in the city get out, and let those in the country not enter the

city. For this is the time of punishment in fulfillment of all that has been written . . . They will fall by the sword and will be taken as prisoners to all the nations. Jerusalem will be trampled on by the Gentiles until the times of the Gentiles are fulfilled" (Luke 21:20-22, 24; emphasis mine).

Here Jesus is clearly speaking of the same events Josephus reported as having occurred during the Great Jewish Revolt. Jerusalem would be surrounded, laid desolate, its people killed or taken into the nations, and Gentiles would lord over Jerusalem for a time. He is speaking about the end of the Jewish age, not the end of the world. The tie in with "let those who are in Judea flee to the mountains . . ." tells us that Jesus was speaking of the same event in Matthew 24 as to what people in Judea should do when they see the "abomination" at the temple—run! The Romans are coming for you next! If Jesus had been speaking of the End Times, what good would it have done to tell people to run for the hills when the world is about to end anyway?

And so, "the abomination that causes desolation" was none other than the setting up of idols and offering of pagan sacrifices by Titus upon the Temple Mount; therefore, Daniel chapter 9 was prophesying about the seven-year tribulation under Rome, not the tribulation of the End Times.

Moses → After this siege, Israel would be scattered to the nations, sent into restless exile and slavery

"Then the Lord will scatter you among all nations, from one end of the earth to the other . . . Among those nations you will find no repose, no resting place for the sole of your foot . . . The Lord will send you back in ships to Egypt on a journey I said you should never make again. There you will offer yourselves for sale to your enemies as male and female slaves, but no one will buy you."
–DEUTERONOMY 28:64-68
(EMPHASIS MINE)

→

During the siege of Jerusalem:

"They [deserters] were all received by the Romans . . . They [the Romans] hoped to get some money by sparing them . . . and sold the rest of the multitude with their wives and children, and every one of them at a very low price, and that because such as were sold were very many, and the buyers were few. . . the number of those that were sold were immense . . ."
–JOSEPHUS, W.J., 6.8.2
(EMPHASIS AND BRACKETS MINE)

JUST AS MOSES PREDICTED, THE ROMANS ENSLAVED SO MANY JEWISH CAPTIVES DURING AND AFTER THE SIEGE THAT THERE WEREN'T EVEN ENOUGH BUYERS ABLE OR WILLING TO BUY THEM UP.

"Then the Lord will <u>scatter you among all nations,</u> from one end of the earth to the other . . . Among those nations <u>you will find no repose,</u> no resting place for the sole of your foot . . . The Lord will <u>send you back in ships to Egypt on a journey I said you should never make again.</u> There you will offer yourselves for sale to your enemies as male and female slaves, but no one will buy you."
–DEUTERONOMY 28:64-68
(EMPHASIS MINE)

→

During the siege of Jerusalem:
". . . as for the rest of the multitude that were above 17 years old, he put them into bonds, and <u>sent them to the Egyptian mines.</u> Titus also <u>sent a great number into the provinces,</u> as a present to them . . . now the number of those carried captive during this whole war was collected 97,000. . . "
–JOSEPHUS, *W.J.,* 6.9.2-6.9.3
(EMPHASIS MINE)

Here Josephus records the fulfillment of Moses' prophecy that the Jews would be scattered all over the world and, specifically, that they would return to Egypt as slaves once more. The Roman Empire at this time was vast, and since Titus couldn't even sell all the Jewish captives, he began sending them all over the empire as mere gifts, spoils of war. Many were likely sold

Schnorr von Carolsfeld, Julius. *The Egyptians Afflicted the Israelites with Burdens.* 1860. www.thefullwiki.org.

beyond even the borders of Rome, judging by how widely dispersed Jews are to this very day.

This "diaspora" of Jews continued through the Second Jewish Revolt (132–136 A.D.) as Rome continued to purge Palestine of all Jews to put an end to their ceaseless rebellion.

Moses → This nation from far away would decimate Israel's cities

"They will lay siege to all the cities throughout your land until the high fortified walls in which you trust fall down. They will besiege all the cities throughout the land the Lord your God is giving you."
–Deuteronomy 28:52

→

The damage toll after the Second Jewish Revolt:

"Fifty of their most important garrisons and 985 of their most renowned towns were blotted out . . . nearly the whole of Judaea was made desolate . . ."
–Cassius Dio, H.R., 5.69.14

Cassius Dio was a Roman historian who wrote Historia Romana, which documented some of the details of the Second Jewish Revolt led by Simon Bar Kokba, starting in 132 A.D. While the Romans laid waste to many cities and towns throughout Israel's land during the first war, General Vespasian also spared many that surrendered out of desire for peace. Here we can see that the second time around, they literally wiped the Jewish civilization off the map. Neither Assyria nor Babylon had wrought such destruction on the Jews as did the Romans. When Moses said all cities throughout Israel would be besieged, he really meant ALL—almost one thousand cities and towns. By 136 A.D., Rome had lived up to their part in this prophecy.

Moses → After the terrible destruction wrought by this far-away country, Israel's population will be decimated.

"You who were as numerous as the stars in the sky will be left but few in number, because you did not obey the Lord your God."
–Deuteronomy 28:62

→

". . . the number of those that perished during the whole siege eleven hundred thousand . . ." [1.1 million]
–Josephus, W.J., 6.9.3 (BRACKETS MINE)

→

"Very few of them survived . . . Fifty-eight myriads of men [580,000] were slaughtered . . . and the number of those that perished by famine and disease and fire was past all investigating."
–Cassius Dio, H.R., 5.69.14 (BRACKETS MINE)

119

Here we have the death accounts of the First, and later, the Second Jewish Revolts. During the 70 A.D. siege of Jerusalem, Josephus reported that the death toll afterward was so high because of the number of Jews coming to celebrate Passover. Titus kept letting people into the city during the early siege, but then would not let them leave after the completion of the festival. This escalated the famine and disease and made them all fish in a barrel for the final assault. Of course, thousands more died in the other sieges and battles around the country during the war.

Cassius Dio reported these casualty numbers after the Second Jewish Revolt that ended around 136 A.D. If this was just the number of men who died in battle, the final death toll of all Jews due to these other factors was likely well over one million again.

One can see how between these two wars, two to four million Jews must have perished at the hands of Rome. The Romans reduced these millions of "stars" to but a few faint lights of despair tossed to the four corners of the earth.

TYING IT ALL TOGETHER

Moses and Daniel predicted and historians affirm that

1. **A mighty nation of IRON from far away, who spoke a language unfamiliar to Israel, would crush the major powers before it and swoop down upon Israel like an eagle** → The Romans came from far away, spoke a very unfamiliar language of Latin, crushed all the kingdoms in that part of the world, swooped down on Israel and subjugated it very quickly, and did so with the symbol of an eagle leading the way.

2. **The ruler of these Romans would make an alliance against Israel for seven years** → Vespasian made an alliance of regional military forces against the Jews, which lasted from 67–74 A.D.

3. **In the middle of these seven years, the temple sacrifice system would come to an end** → This occurred during the Roman siege of Jerusalem in 70 A.D.

4. **After this, an abomination would be set up on a wing of the temple** → Prince Titus and his soldiers offered up pagan sacrifices to his Roman "ensigns" on the Temple Mount.

5. **Jerusalem and the temple would be destroyed** → Titus gave the order to level the city and the temple in the September of 70 A.D.

6. **All of Israel's cities would be destroyed** → The Romans destroyed over one thousand Israeli cities and garrisons over the course of two wars.

7. **The Jews would once again be sold as slaves in Egypt** → Rome shipped many Jewish captives from Jerusalem to Egypt to work in the mines.

8. **The Jewish population would be decimated; the surviving remnant scattered across the world** → Josephus and Cassius Dio confirmed this happened over the course of two great wars with Rome.

And so, the judgmental curse which God promised to Israel through Moses was completely fulfilled, as predicted in the books of Deuteronomy and Daniel at least two hundred years before it actually happened (likely hundreds of years earlier than that). For their years of sinful living in violation of their covenant with God and their rejection of his Son, Jesus, he punished their evil and flung the Jews to the far reaches of the earth as he warned them he would.

Once again, we have a case of prophecy actually predicting some very specific and timely events hundreds of years before they happened. Predictions down to within a month in the case of the timing of the war and ending of sacrifices. How could the prophets have known the details of Israel's doom so far in advance? Once again, this is strong evidence for a divine hand on the Bible—it is highly improbable that all these specific predictions could have just been lucky guesswork. There was certainly no way that the Jews could have manipulated world events to result in the fulfillment of all these prophecies in such a specific way—who would wish that kind of suffering and devastation upon themselves anyway!

But prophecy is not done telling the story of Israel just yet. God is still working his plan. The prophets spoke of a new dawn for their nation after this Great Tribulation—the dawning of a day that would bring us to "the Last Days" of Earth.

ISRAEL REBORN

"You will arise and have compassion on Zion,
for it is time to show favor to her; the appointed time has come . . .
For the Lord will rebuild Zion and appear in His glory."
—PSALM 102:13, 16

After the Great Tribulation of 70 A.D., the Jews found themselves decimated and scattered to the four winds of the earth. With God's Temple destroyed, and the sacrificial system of Judaism with it, Christianity was able to break free from its Jewish roots and flourish as the New Covenant with God through his Son, Jesus Christ. Rome erased the geopolitical nation of Israel from the earth, and for the next 1,900 years, Jerusalem laid in the hands of the Gentiles as Jesus and the prophets foretold. And yet, throughout this whole time, the City of God remained one of the most desired pieces of real estate on Earth.

But the nation of Israel did not completely die at the hands of Rome—it lived on in the hearts and minds of every Jew who survived Rome's great purge. The Jewish people became restless wanderers and faced persecution among the nations, as Moses had warned them. The reality of the prophets hit home in a very real way; the Israelites had failed to heed their warnings, and God's judgment could not be escaped. Yet the Jewish people persevered over the centuries with the rise and fall of entire nations, religions, and ideologies all around them. They flourished and continued to grow as a people all over the world until the dawn of the twentieth century saw their return to center stage. They suffered one of their greatest tragedies at the hands of Nazi Germany, but thereafter received one of their greatest victories—the return of their nation, Israel . . . their Promised Land . . . their home.

As we will see, however, this welcomed return was no mere coincidence; it was orchestrated by God himself. This future restoration of Israel was made known to his people through the prophets as a message of hope in dark times and as a sign of "the Last Days," which would usher in the reign of the Messiah on Earth. For those that believe Jesus is the Messiah, this will be his return to claim those who love him and to establish his kingdom. Let us now unfold the Old Testament prophecy and the history behind the rebirth of this special nation, Israel.

FROM ALIYAH TO A NATION

Fast forward from the second century to the late nineteenth century. Jewish populations existed in the millions all over the world, living amongst foreign nations and holding onto hopes of the future. It was at this time, however, when the Jewish people began to reawaken to their desires to be one people and one nation under God once more. What follows is a short summary of the last 130 years of Jewish history.

History of Israel

136 A.D.
The Romans quell the Bar Kokhba Revolt. They purge Israel of Jews and wipe their cities off the map. Israel as a geopolitical nation is no more.

1882–1903 A.D.
The First Aliyah. Jews throughout western Russia come under persecution through a series of anti-Semetic "pogroms" or riots. These were inflamed by a number of socioeconomic factors. Feeling that only a return to their homeland will bring about security, around twenty-five thousand Jews, mainly from Poland and Ukraine, make "aliyah," or ascent, to the Promised Land (called Palestine at the time). They purchase around ninety thousand acres of land and found twenty-eight new settlements. The Hebrew language reemerges in their land once more and comes to be taught in their new schools (Jewish Agency).

1904–1914 A.D.
The Second Aliyah. After a period of stagnation, a second round of Russian pogroms combined with new nationalistic fervor (Zionism) motivate a young, enthusiastic group of Jews to begin migrating to their homeland. During this decade, around forty thousand of these pioneers establish a new working class in Palestine and lay the foundation of Tel Aviv—the first all-Jewish city in centuries. They continue to nourish Hebrew culture and literature. They also begin to develop a Jewish defense force. The aliyah is interrupted by the outbreak of World War I (Jewish Agency).

1919–1923 A.D.
The Third Aliyah. A fresh Zionist movement arises out of WWI and the following Bolshevik Revolution in Russia. The British government gains control of Palestine through the League of Nations and makes known its desire to establish a Jewish state in the . . .

1924–1928 A.D.
The Fourth Aliyah. The migration of Jews from Soviet Russia becomes restricted, however, sixty-seven thousand Jews immigrate to Palestine—around half from Poland (Jewish Agency).

History of Israel

1919–1923 A.D. (cont'd)

territory. This renewed hope brought another thirty thousand Jews to Palestine from eastern Europe and Russia during this period. They continue to make developments in Jewish industry, construction, defense, and agriculture (Jewish Agency).

1929–1939 A.D.

The Fifth Aliyah. Adolf Hitler rises to power during this time and begins to persecute the Jews in Germany and later, Austria. A massive exodus of around 250,000 Jews from all over Europe brings the Jewish population of Palestine up to around half a million (Jewish Agency).

1939–1945 A.D.

The Holocaust. Hitler unleashes his Nazi war machine upon Europe and quickly claims large swaths of territory in the opening days of World War II. Overwhelmed by the absorption of so many Jews in these lands, the Nazis initiate the systematic killing of Jews, first by death squads, then by death camps. By the end of the war, Germany was responsible for the slaughter of more than six million Jews (Britannica 2014, "Holocaust").

1947 A.D.

The war ends, and as the horrors of the Holocaust come to light, the floodgates are opened for Jewish immigration to Palestine. As tensions mount between Jews and Arabs over the influx of these refugees, Britain appeals to the United Nations (UN) for assistance. The General Assembly votes to divide Palestine into two states—one Jewish, one Arab (Britannica 2014, "Israel").

1948 A.D.

Israel Reborn. Under the leadership of David Ben-Gurion, Israel declares its nationhood and independence from Britain under the UN mandate, upheld by international recognition. The new nation immediately comes under assault from Egypt, Iraq, Lebanon, Syria, and Jordan. The Zionist forces miraculously repel the invaders and secure their new homeland, the State of Israel (Britannica 2014, "Israel").

1967 A.D.

The Six Day War. Tensions between Israel and its Arab neighbors lead to massing of their forces in preparation for war. Surrounded, Israel conducts a crippling surprise attack on Egypt and destroys its air force on the ground. In six days, Israel routes Egypt, Syria, and Jordan, and claims the Suez Canal, the West Bank, the Golan Heights, and most importantly, Jerusalem (Britannica 2014, "Israel").

History of Israel

1967–Present

Peace between Israel and the Arab world remains elusive. Conflicts between Israel and its neighbors plague the region, especially with the growth of radical Islam and the rise of their numerous extremist groups. In spite of all this, Israel has flourished militarily, economically, and socially. It has become a beacon for democracy and freedom in the Middle East. With international aid and self-determination, Israel has become a powerful nation to be dealt with in the Middle East.

Over the last five decades, millions of Jews have immigrated to Israel from all over the world. The Jewish population of Israel now numbers over six million, with many more Jews continuing to make "aliyah" to their homeland each year. The one aspect of their culture yet to be resurrected is the reinstitution of Mosaic Law through the rebuilding of the Temple of God. Demand for its reconstruction increases, as does Muslim resistance to Israeli influence over the Temple Mount. It is a flashpoint for inevitable wars to come.

THE VOICES OF THE PROPHETS AND THE REBIRTH OF ISRAEL

Since its inception, the young nation of Israel has quickly become central to world politics and events. Its struggle is a great story, ongoing in the pages of modern history. Would it surprise you, then, to know that Israel's story was already written on the pages of Scripture more than two thousand years ago? Through despair, captivity, and persecution, God spoke encouragement to his people through his prophets, that in spite of their sufferings, he would one day restore them like never before. That day has come, and the voices of the prophets time and again jump off the pages of Scripture into the headlines of history.

Jeremiah → In spite of being scattered to the world, the national identity of Israel will endure

> "'So do not be afraid, Jacob my servant; do not be dismayed,
> Israel,' declares the Lord . . . 'I am with you and will save you . . .
> Though I completely destroy all the nations among which I scatter you,
> I will not completely destroy you.'"
> —JEREMIAH 30:10,11 (EMPHASIS MINE)

As mentioned earlier, for almost two thousand years the Jews were wanderers amongst the lands of other peoples and religions. Their enemies hoped that by dispersing them throughout the world, they would be assimilated into other populations and cease to be a nation capable of resistance. But the people of Israel endured across the millennia and maintained their identity, their language, and their faith. Nations and empires rose and fell all around them, but the chosen people of God outlasted them all by God's grace and divine plan.

© Emyerson. 2006. Istockphoto.com

The Prophets → After worldwide exile, Israel will be restored to their homeland and prosper

> *"When all these blessings and curses I have set before you come on you and you take them to heart <u>wherever the Lord your God disperses you among the nations</u>, and when you and your children return to the Lord your God . . . then the Lord your God will restore your fortunes and have compassion on you and <u>gather you again from all the nations where he scattered you</u>. Even if you have been banished to the most distant land under the heavens, from there the Lord your God will gather you and bring you back. He will <u>bring you to the land that belonged to your ancestors</u>, and you will take possession of it. <u>He will make you more prosperous and numerous than your ancestors</u>."*
> –DEUTERONOMY 30:1-5 (EMPHASIS MINE)

Only two chapters after Moses informed Israel that they would be destroyed and scattered across the world by a faraway nation (Rome), he revealed that the story would not end there. Here, God promised that once the people of Israel have had time to reflect on their sin and turn their hearts back to him, he would finally restore them to great prosperity in their land—more so than ever before. We know this prophecy does not speak of the return from Babylonian exile because 1) it was to occur *after* Rome came; 2) the Babylonian exile was localized to the Mediterranean/Fertile Crescent region, not "the most distant land under the heavens"; and 3) the Jews did not at that time take possession of their land as this Scripture indicates would happen—the Promised Land remained under foreign control from the coming of Babylon until the twentieth century.

This prophecy became a reality in 1948 when the nation state of Israel was finally restored and repossessed by the Jewish people. Since that time, more than three million Jews have made aliyah to their homeland from all over the world (Bard 2014, "Immigration"); their numbers have grown to over six million total as of 2014 (Jerusalem Institute 2014, "Population").

The question does remain, however—did the Jews and/or their children return to the Lord before he restored their nation? While I have been unable to find definitive data of the overall religious identity of those thousands of Jews who immigrated to Israel after its restoration, the percentage of God-followers in today's Israeli society indicates that a good number of those returning must have clung to Jewish religion/traditions.

A survey of 2,803 Israeli Jews conducted by the Guttman Center in 2009 provides some insight as to what extent Israeli Jews are returning to God. As a foundational statistic, 80 percent expressed belief in God and over 65 percent believed that Jews are God's chosen people and that the Law (Torah) is God given. The idea that modern Israel is largely atheist is absolutely wrong. The decade between 1999 and 2009 showed a slow but steady increase in beliefs and religious practices of Israeli Jews in spite of a large influx of more secular Jews from the prior Soviet Union in the 90s. Around 54 percent, up from 49 percent, hold traditional or more fundamental religious views. 84 percent, up from 78 percent, observe Jewish religious traditions at least to some extent, with 40 percent seriously observing them (Guttman 2009). This means that a growing majority of Israelites are turning their hearts back to God. The foundation is certainly there for Judaism to return in its full temple form (more on this later). And so, the condition of this prophecy for Jews to return to God seems to be finding ongoing fulfillment in the descendants of the Holocaust generation as they steadily rediscover their religious roots.

> "'The days are coming,' declares the Lord, 'when I will bring my people Israel and Judah back from captivity and restore them to the land I gave their ancestors to possess,' says the Lord . . . In that day, declares the Lord Almighty, '<u>I will break the yoke off their necks and will tear off their bonds; no longer will foreigners enslave them.</u>'"
>
> —JEREMIAH 30:3, 8 (EMPHASIS MINE)

Not only did Jeremiah also foretell the Jews' return to the Promised Land, he assured them that they would one day finally be free from foreign rule. The prophet hits the mark again as the people of Israel had been under foreign rule since the Babylonians subjugated Judah and took them into exile. (While a portion of Judah won their freedom from the Seleucid Empire in 167 B.C., it was certainly not representative of the whole nation. By 63 B.C., Judah was subjugated once more, this time by the Romans.) Now, after more than 2,500 years, Israel stands as a sovereign nation—free from foreign control once more.

> "In that day the Lord will reach out his hand a second time to reclaim the surviving remnant of his people from Assyria, from Lower Egypt, from Upper Egypt, from Cush, from Elam, from Babylonia, from Hamath and from the islands of the Mediterranean. He will raise a banner for the nations and gather the exiles of Israel; he will assemble the scattered people of Judah from the four quarters of the earth."
>
> —ISAIAH 11:11-12

"In that day" is set in the context of the time after the Messiah comes (v. 10), so we know this verse cannot be referring to any instance of Jews returning to their homeland before that time. We also know this is referring to the twentieth century aliyah because Isaiah mentions that this would be the second time that the Jews would return from foreign exile. As we've seen, there has only been one other such return from captivity, which took place after Persia freed the Jews from Babylon.

"Though I [God] scatter them [Israel] among the peoples,
yet in distant lands they will remember me.
They and their children will survive, and they will return."
–ZECHARIAH 10:9 (BRACKETS MINE)

"This is what the Sovereign Lord says: 'I will take the Israelites out of
the nations where they have gone. I will gather them from all around
and bring them back into their own land.'"
–EZEKIEL 37:21

Here we know Zechariah must also have been speaking of a future re-gathering of Israel, because he was part of the remnant of Jews already freed from captivity to return to their homeland and rebuild (the first re-gathering). In general, we also know that all of these prophets were speaking of a future return of Israel (not the return from Babylonian exile), because they assert that the Jews will be scattered to many distant nations, to "the four quarters of the earth." Again, the Babylonian dispersion only scattered Jews throughout the Mediterranean region.

This makes at least five biblical prophets over the centuries that knew Israel would be scattered across the world and then returned to their land in the future (others make mention of this fact as well). No other nation can claim to have returned to existence once wiped off the map and its people purged from their land. What's more is that no other nation has ever known thousands of years in advance that such a restoration would actually happen. How is it that all five of these men could have known without the foresight of God that circumstances two thousand years later would come together to allow their nation and their people to be restored? More lucky guesswork? These men were confident that all these things would happen just the way they said—and they did!

Isaiah → Israel would be born in a day

"Before she [Jerusalem] goes into labor, she gives birth; before the pains
come upon her, she delivers a son. Who has ever heard of such things?

> *Who has ever seen things like this?* <u>*Can a country be born in a day or*</u>
> <u>*a nation be brought forth in a moment?*</u> *Yet no sooner is Zion in labor*
> *than she gives birth to her children . . . Rejoice with Jerusalem and be*
> *glad for her . . . all you who mourn over her . . . you will drink deeply*
> *and delight in her <u>overflowing abundance</u>*
> —Isaiah 66:7-11 (emphasis and brackets mine)

Jerusalem was (and still is) the center of the Jewish world, culture, and faith even though the physical nation of Israel had not existed for almost two thousand years. Here Isaiah painted a picture of Jerusalem as a mother for an entire nation yet to be born—it's people, scattered around the globe, were still connected to the city which they held most dear. Out of the womb of mother Jerusalem, a new nation came into being—it just so happens that the modern State of Israel *was* born in a day!

> MAY 14, 1948
> *"By virtue of the natural and historic right of the Jewish*
> *people and by resolution of the General Assembly of the*
> *United Nations, we hereby proclaim the establishment of*
> *a Jewish state in Palestine to be called Israel."*
> —David Ben-Gurion, former Leader of
> Jewish National Council (Cavendish 1998)

Above left: © KCHL. Israeli flag. 2014. Istockphoto. com. Below: Kluger Zoltan. Israel Declaration of Independence. 1948. Israeli Government Press Office.

The UN granted Israel its existence in the previous year through Resolution 181. On May 14, 1948, when Israel finally declared its independence, many nations instantly recognized it as a sovereign nation, giving it full nation status in a day. Before this day, the land was simply known as Palestine.

It is even more amazing to note Isaiah's analogy of the circumstances surrounding Israel's rebirth. Many nations are formed or earn their freedom from other countries via conflict (here symbolized as "labor") before they can become independent and later recognized as a self-governing state ("birth" of a new country). In Israel's case, however, they were first recognized as a state and granted independence (born) and then went to war with five Arabic nations the very next day to fight for its existence (labor). Isaiah was on target with this analogy.

Isaiah also predicted here that Israel would "drink" in Jerusalem's abundance after their nation was reborn. Since Israel reclaimed Jerusalem from Jordan in 1967, they have been prospering greatly. The wealth generated from millions of tourists to Jerusalem each year contributes substantially to their economic growth. In 2013 alone, over 3.5 million visitors to Israel generated around $11.4 billion for Israel's economy—an estimated 75 percent of these visitors spent time in Jerusalem (Yaakov 2014). All three aspects of this prophecy have been fulfilled in the formation and growth of the modern State of Israel.

Ezekiel → Israel would complete its punishment for sin in 1948

This is a more complicated prophecy than most and ties in more than one section of Scripture; but like the prophecy in Daniel 9 foretelling Jesus' arrival to Jerusalem in 33 A.D., the mathematical precision with which this prophecy is made is worth the effort to understand it.

Summary of Ezekiel 4

In this chapter, Ezekiel was prophesying to the Jewish exiles in Babylon, warning them about the coming destruction of Jerusalem at the hands of their captors. This was to be a judgment for their peoples' ongoing sins. God told Ezekiel to make a mock-up of Jerusalem under siege as a sign to Israel of things to come. Then he directed him to lie next to it for a total of 430 days, symbolizing the bearing of 430 years of Israel's sin. During this whole time, he was to prophesy against the mock up, as if against Jerusalem and eat unclean bread, as the Jews would do in the nations they were to be banished to for this 430-year time period. "In this way the people of Israel will eat defiled food among the nations where I [God] will drive them" (Ezek. 4:13; brackets mine).

So, Israel will bear their sins amongst the nations for 430 years. When did this period begin? Jeremiah gives us some insight:

> "Because you [Judah] have not listened to my words . . .
> This whole country [Israel] will become a desolate wasteland,
> and these nations will serve the king of Babylon 70 years."
> —JEREMIAH 25:8,11 (BRACKETS MINE)

Unknown Artist. *Prophet Ezekiel.*
Accessed October 27, 2014. www.christianimagesource.com.

These verses tell us that the sins of Israel were ultimately laid on Judah, so the timing of their punishment amongst the nations started with them. Here, Jeremiah revealed that the people of Israel would be exiled to Babylon for a period of 70 years—their time amongst the nations started with the first exile to Babylon in 606 B.C. as we saw in chapter 1.

1) Start the clock at 606 B.C.→Fast forward 70 years:

As with the Daniel 9 prophecy in chapter 2, we must convert 70 Prophetic years of 360 days to Gregorian years of 365.25 days:

70 years x 360 days per year = 25,200 days →25,200 days / 365.25 days per year = **69 Gregorian years of exile to Babylon** 606 B.C. – 69 years = **537 B.C.**

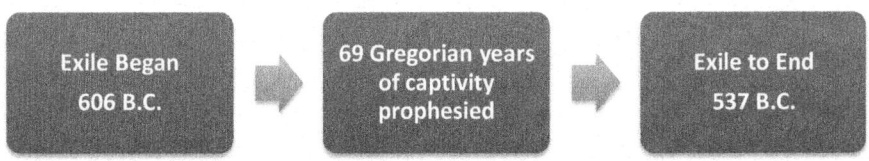

As we saw earlier, this was the year in which Persia released the first wave of Jews from captivity to return and start rebuilding the Holy Temple. While many Jews eventually returned to Israel to rebuild, still many others remained in Babylon, or in the other nations around the Mediterranean, to which they had fled. Their time of iniquity amongst the nations continued and of course would later be brought upon them in full force by the Romans. But what about the remaining time of this prophecy?

430 years − 70 years = **360 years** of bearing sin amongst the nations remaining

Convert 360 to Gregorian years, and this only brings us to 182 B.C. At this time the Jews were still nowhere near completing their time of iniquity amongst the nations—they were still under the heel of Greek rule and slated to be destroyed and scattered even more severely by the Romans about 250 years later. So, did God lie to Israel? Or is there something else going on here? We must dig far back into Scripture to find the answer.

2) The key to the remaining time lies in the book of Leviticus, chapter 26. Moses started this chapter by relaying God's Word to Israel about the blessings they would receive from God if they obeyed his covenant. But, as usual, with blessings came warnings and curses:

"But if you will not listen to me and carry out all these commands . . . and so violate my covenant, then I will do this to you: I will bring on you sudden terror . . . You will plant seed in vain, because your enemies will eat it. I will set my face against you so that you will be defeat-

> *ed by your enemies; those you hate you will rule over you, and you will flee even when no one is pursuing you. If after all this you will not listen to me, <u>I will punish you for your sins **seven times over**</u> . . . I will turn your cities into ruins and lay waste your sanctuaries. . . I will scatter you among the nations and will draw out my sword and pursue you . . ."*
> —LEVITICUS 26:14-32 (EMPHASIS MINE)

This is only the abbreviated version of this text. If you read these verses in their entirety, God revealed many horrors that would be visited on Israel for their disobedience. He continued to reiterate that if these punishments did not sway them from their sins, then the punishment would be multiplied **seven times**. He repeated this pattern throughout this section. This means that whatever length of punishment God had ordained for Israel, he promised it would be visited upon them seven times over if they continued to disobey. So, when the Jews throughout the world failed to fully return to God's covenant after their release from exile in 537 B.C., God extended their remaining punishment of 360 years by seven times:

360 years x 7 = 2,520 additional years of bearing iniquity → Convert to Gregorian years (See Daniel 9 prophecy in chapter 2) = **2,484 years**

Total Time of Bearing Iniquity = 2484 + 69 = **2553 Gregorian years**

2553 years – 606 B.C. = 1947 A.D. → Add 1 year, because there is no year zero, and we arrive at:

We arrive at the very year when Israel as a whole nation was reborn, and its people finally able to freely return home from their worldwide exile. Leviticus 26 concluded with the final hope that once Israel's sins had been paid living amongst the nations and that once the land of Israel had enjoyed its Sabbath rests, God would uphold his covenant with Abraham and make them a mighty nation in the Promised Land once more. In 1948, Israel's mandated punishment and exile came to an end, and they have been streaming back home ever since.

God *always* keeps his Word, and this case was no different: he warned Israel, they disobeyed; he set a time for punishment and exile; afterward, they continued to disobey; he multiplied their punishment and exile by seven times as he promised; and it all came to an end in 1948, exactly when he said it would.

As the "icing on the cake" of God's perfection in all this, it's amazing to note that there were 19 years between the first exile of Judah in 606 B.C. and the destruction of Jerusalem in 587 B.C.—it just so happens that there were also 19 years between the restoration of Israel in 1948 and their reclamation of Jerusalem in 1967. The circle of Israel's formation, punishment, and restoration is now complete in God's perfect time!

Isaiah/Ezekiel → After gathering Israel from the nations, they will be united as one nation

As we learned in chapter 1, when Israel's King Solomon died, the nation of Israel was divided into two nations—Israel in the north and Judah to the south. It remained this way until Assyria obliterated Israel and subjugated Judah. Since those times, Israel has not existed as a full nation, united under one leader—until now. This, too, was part of Israel's future story foretold by the prophets.

Isaiah speaking of the time when God would gather his people from the nations:

> *"Ephraim's jealousy will vanish, and Judah's enemies will be destroyed; Ephraim will not be jealous of Judah, nor Judah hostile toward Ephraim."*
> –ISAIAH 11:13

Here, Isaiah was referring to the northern kingdom of Israel as "Ephraim," the most prominent of the ten northern tribes. In those days of the divided kingdom, Israel and Judah were often in conflict with one another. Their kings did not like to "play nice" together most of the time. Today, however, all descendants of the twelve tribes of Israel live in peace and cooperation with one another as a single nation once more.

Ezekiel prophesying on the same event:

> "This is what the Sovereign Lord says: 'I will take the Israelites out of the nations where they have gone. I will gather them from all around and bring them back into their own land. I will make them one nation in the land, on the mountains of Israel. There will be one king over all of them and they will never again be two nations or be divided into two kingdoms.'"
> –EZEKIEL 37:21-22 (EMPHASIS MINE)

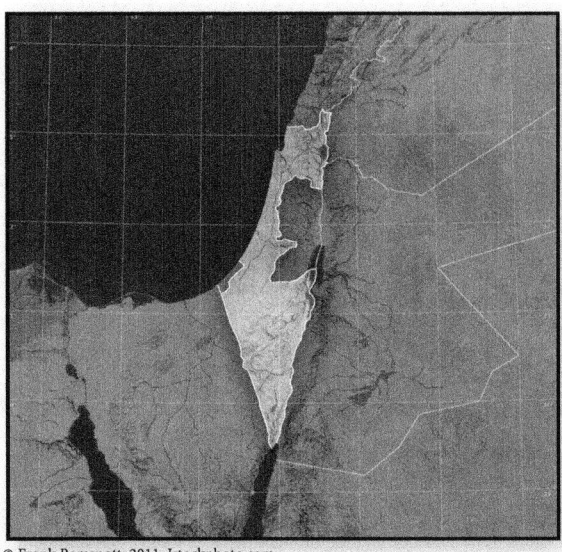

© Frank Ramspott. 2011. Istockphoto.com.

And so it is today—Israel is under a single ruler (here called "king" because ancient Jews would have had no concept of a modern "prime minister"). From the time of the Divided Kingdom until 1948, Israel has not existed as one nation, only in smaller pieces under mostly foreign rulers. The people of Israel are one again, united in their zeal to thrive in their homeland.

Hosea/Jeremiah→After years without a ruler, Israel will return in the Last Days under the rule of "David"

> *"For the Israelites <u>will live many days without king or prince,</u> without sacrifice or sacred stones, without ephod or household gods. <u>Afterward the Israelites will return and seek the Lord their God and David their king.</u> They will come trembling to the Lord and to his blessings <u>in the last days.</u>"*
> –HOSEA 3:4-5 (EMPHASIS MINE)

> *"'In that day,' declares the Lord Almighty, 'I will break the yoke off their necks and will tear off their bonds; no longer will foreigners enslave them. Instead, <u>they will serve the Lord their God and David their king, whom I will raise up for them.</u>'"*
> –JEREMIAH 30:8-9 (EMPHASIS MINE)

As we know, up until 1948, the Israelites had lived for over 2,500 years under foreign rule and for almost 2,000 years without a temple in which to conduct sacrifices. These prophecies assert that after this period, when the Israelites returned to their land and finally gained their independence from foreign control, their ruler would be named David. It just so happened that the modern State of Israel was founded under the leadership of one David-Ben Gurion—their first prime minister. After that day, Jews from all over the world began to return to their homeland to "seek the Lord their God and David their king." At no time since the orig-inal King David of ancient Israel has there been another Israeli rul-er of that name, so we know that these prophecies could only have been pointing to modern times. Is it coincidence that the founder of modern Israel bore the same name as the king that established the first kingdom of Israel? Or divine prov-idence?

David Ben-Gurion. 1952. Israeli Govern-ment Press Office.

At first glance, it might seem as if these prophecies could be referring to the return after the

139

Babylonian exile, but the context just doesn't fit. While the returning Babylonian remnant did live many days without king or sacrifices and did return to the Promised Land seeking God, they did not have a king to return to and they were not free of foreign subjugation.

Some think "David" might refer to "Jesus," since he was the promised descendant of King David. This is the case with some prophetic Scriptures, but it does not fit the context of these verses. The Jews largely rejected Jesus at his first coming—they were not seeking him. Plus, in the times of Jesus, priests were conducting sacrifices to God at Herod's temple, and Israel was under the heel of Rome—the situation was quite the opposite of the conditions described in these verses. The only situation that takes into account all of the context behind these two prophecies is the return from the worldwide exile to an independent State of Israel, under the leadership of David Ben-Gurion, in the mid twentieth century.

Jeremiah→After the Jews return from the nations, God will put shepherds over them, and they will no longer be afraid

> "'I, myself, will gather the remnant of my flock out of all the countries where I have driven them bring them back to their pasture, where they will be fruitful and increase in number. I will place shepherds over them who will tend to them, and they will no longer be afraid or terrified, nor will any be missing,' declares the Lord."
> –JEREMIAH 23:3-4 (EMPHASIS MINE)

Since the people of Israel have returned to their "pasture," many nations have looked out for them and provided aid, but of course none of these stand above the shepherding protection of the United States. The US has been Israel's ally since the beginning and in recent years has solidified its status as Israel's primary "shepherd." Since Israel's inception in 1948, the U.S. has provided them over $121 billion in total aid [no adjustment for inflation] (Sharp 2014, 2). The US has also supplied countless small arms as well as modern aircraft and armor and has assisted Israel with research and development of their own weapons systems, such as the Iron Dome. Recently, the United

States made a strong statement of support in declaring Israel a major strategic partner through passing of the "United States-Israel Strategic Partnership Act of 2014," which lays out cooperation in areas such as defense, research, energy, and security (AIPAC 2014). Israel's survival and security is greatly reliant on the support of the United States, and because of that support, they are no longer afraid of foreign opposition—they meet it head on.

Isaiah→The sons and daughters of Israel will return to their homeland through the air

God speaking to Zion (Israel):

> *"All assemble and come to you; your sons come from afar, your daughters are carried on the hip . . . Who are these that fly along like clouds, like doves to their nests?"*
> –ISAIAH 60:4, 8

Speaking of the future return of the people of Israel, Isaiah predicted that they would return via the clouds, flying like doves to their nests (which implies they are going home). It's no secret that Jews from all over the world have been returning to their homeland in droves via the sky over the last century. The context of this chapter makes little room for misinterpretation—Isaiah predicted that one day his people would fly home!

Isaiah → A nation to the north and to the south of Israel will resist letting their Jewish citizens return home

> *"Do not be afraid, for I am with you [Israel]; I will bring your children from the east and gather you from the west. <u>I will say to the north, 'Give them up!' and to the south, 'Do not hold them back.'</u> Bring my sons from afar and my daughters from the ends of the earth."*
> –ISAIAH 43:5-6 (EMPHASIS MINE)

After Israel became an independent nation, Jews from all over the world were able to freely return to their ancient homeland. These verses seem to indicate, however, that a land to the north of Israel and a land to its south would resist giving up their Jews when God called them home from the nations. It just so happens that both the Soviet Union (to the north) and Ethiopia (to the south) were very resistant to allowing their Jews to return to Israel after its rebirth in 1948.

The Soviet Aliyah

The Soviet Union (USSR) was THE country to the north of Israel (and all other Asian nations, for that matter). For the USSR to be the country to the "north" in this prophecy makes perfect sense, as many Jews were trapped behind the Iron Curtain by the time Israel once again became a state. From 1948 to 1970, only around 21,000 Jews were able to leave the USSR for Israel (whether legally or illegally). During the 1960s, only 4,000 Jews were legally allowed to emigrate due to Soviet politics and persecution. During the 1970s, a combination of international pressure and internal Jewish emigration movements coerced the USSR to finally open its gates, allowing over 156,000 Jews to return to Israel in that decade. Then, in the two decades following the fall of the Iron Curtain in 1990, almost one million Jews flooded out of Soviet countries to the Promised Land (Jewish Agency 2009; Alekseyeva 1983).

Soviet "refuseniks" demonstrating. 1973. En.wikipedia.org.

The Ethiopian Aliyah

Ethiopia lies several nations south of Israel at the opposite end of the Red Sea. From the seventeenth century up through the 1980s, the Jewish population of this country was subject to persecution, were

Tsvika, Israeli. Operation Solomon.
1991. Israeli Government Press Office.

considered outcasts, and were denied the practice of their religion. What's worse is that they were not even allowed to leave Ethiopia to escape the oppression—those caught trying to leave during the mid 1900s were killed for it.

From 1980 to 1985, Israel conducted covert Operations Moses and Joshua to smuggle around 8,000 Jews into Israel through Kenya and Sudan (Ministry of Aliyah 1984). The CIA even chimed in to extract around 500 refugees from Sudan (Bard 2015, "Ethiopia"). In 1990, Israel and the Ethiopian government finally came to accord with the Family Reunification Agreement, which allowed for about 1,000 Jews to leave for Israel per month.

The following year, however, many Jewish refugees trying to leave the country came under threat from Ethiopian rebels. In response, Israel initiated Operation Solomon to airlift over 14,000 Jews in thirty-six hours. Over the next couple decades, some 43,000 were able to make aliyah, and by 2013 the number of Ethiopian Jews returned to Israel reached 125,000 after three decades of effort (JVL, "Ethiopia"; Sales 2013).

And so, the USSR to the north of Israel and Ethiopia to the south had to be coerced into releasing their Jews as this prophecy foretold. Not even the Soviet Union could keep God's people from heeding his call to return home.

Isaiah → After Israel's return from worldwide exile, they will be empowered by God, grow in strength, and will destroy their enemies

> *"But you, Israel . . . I took you from the ends of the earth, from its farthest corners I called you . . . So do not fear, for I am with you . . . I will strengthen you and help you; I will uphold you with my righteous right hand. All who rage against you will surely be ashamed and disgraced; those who oppose you will be as nothing and perish . . . Those who wage war against you will be as nothing at all. For I am the Lord your God who takes hold of your right hand and says to you, Do not fear; I will help you . . . I will make you into a threshing sledge, new and sharp, with many teeth."*
> —ISAIAH 41:8-16 (EMPHASIS MINE)

Photos courtesy of www.idfblog.com and israeli-weapons.com.

And, oh, the "teeth" Israel has now! With the aid of numerous countries since their inception, Israel is stronger militarily than it ever was in the past. They have received a vast array of modern weaponry through cooperation with the United States, and now even produce their own tanks (some of the best in the world), firearms, missile defense systems, and other military technology.

A quick glance at Globalfirepower.com reveals Israel's growing status as a world military power. Here are their military specs as of 2015:

Active Duty: 160,000 (#35 in the world)

Reserves: 630,000 (#15)

Tanks: 4,170 (#8)

Mechanized Infantry: 10,185 (#4)

Fighters/Strike Aircraft: 242 (#12)

Attack Helicopters: 48 (#11)

THIS EQUALS LOTS OF NEW, SHARP TEETH (especially for a country their size and young age).

Israel is a highly militarized country in which almost all male and female citizens of a certain age much serve in the military for two to three years, with few exceptions. The Israeli Defense Force (IDF) is a battle-tested, highly trained military that has fought against conventional and nonconventional enemies alike. As of 2014, the IDF was ranked number one military in the Middle East by *Business Insider* over countries such as Syria, Turkey, Saudi Arabia, and Jordan due to its experience, technological advantages, training standards, and in particular, its air force and nuclear weapons (Bender 2014). God has truly remade Israel into a nation not to be trifled with.

"All who rage against you will surely be ashamed and disgraced; those who oppose you will be as nothing and perish . . . Those who wage war against you will be as nothing at all . . . " (Isa. 41:11-12).

Such has been the result of Israel's newfound military might. This section of Isaiah's prophecy has come true repeatedly throughout modern Israel's history, as they have struggled against all of its neighbors in numerous conflicts. An unbelievably high kill ratio between Israel and its enemies during the major conflicts reveals just how much Israel has "disgraced" them over the years:

Conflict	Synopsis	Israel Deaths	Adversary Deaths	Israel/Enemy Kill Ratio
1948: War of Independence[1]	One-day-old Israel repelled Egypt, Iraq, Jordan, Syria, Lebanon, and Saudi Arabia, who hated the idea of a Jewish state.	5,800	Approx. 14,400	2.5 to 1
1956: Suez Crisis[2]	Israel, aided by Britain and France, moved to liberate the Suez Canal, which Egypt had on lockdown.	189	2650 (1650 military)	14 to 1
1967: Six Day War[3]	Surrounded on all sides, Israel surprised and dominated Egypt, Syria, Jordan, and Iraq; took Sinai Peninsula, Gaza Strip, West Bank, Golan Heights, and Jerusalem.	800	16,150 to 21,150 (military)	20 or 26 to 1
1969: War of Attrition	Egypt, along with intervention from PLO, Jordan, USSR, Cuba, and Syria, tried to take Sinai back—Israel kept it.	1,424	5,000	3.5 to 1
1973: Yom Kippur War[4]	Israel repelled yet another attempt by Egypt, Syria, Jordan, and Iraq to reclaim territory.	2,656	8,500– 15,000	3 or 5.5 to 1
1982: First Lebanon War	Israel invaded southern Lebanon in response to an assassination attempt on an Israeli ambassador and to expel forces threatening Israel.	1,216	20,825	17 to 1
2006: Second Lebanon War	Israel invaded southern Lebanon in response to Hezbollah aggression.	164	1,954	12 to 1

Table 4.1 Primary data source unless otherwise noted: Bard, "Vital Statistics: Total Casualties, Arab-Israeli Conflict," which was derived from multiple sources. "Israel" and "Adversary Deaths" in most cases include civilian deaths as well due to difficulty in separating civilian from military deaths of Arab countries. "Adversary Deaths" are best estimates in most cases as Arab sources have been difficult to verify.
1. Casualty numbers from Morris 2008, 406-7.
2. Casualty numbers from Varble 2003, 91.
3. Casualty numbers from Oren 2002, 305.
4. Casualty number from Rabinovich 2004, 497.

Across all of the major Israeli-Arab conflicts, Israel maintains an average kill ratio with their enemies as high as 11.5 to 1! Not to mention the extremely lopsided numbers in favor of Israel regarding aircraft, armor warfare, and in some cases, POWs. Further significance can be seen in this ratio when we realize that Israel was greatly outnumbered in every conflict except the two most recent, which were fought against militant organizations, not conventional militaries. Also worthy of note is that while some political stalemates have occurred, Israel has never outright lost a conflict militarily. While this kill ratio is by no means a comprehensive representation of all factors of warfare, it does prove one thing—none of Israel's enemies have been able to stand against them. Ethical and political discussions aside, right or wrong, over the last sixty-seven years, Israel has truly shamed all of their neighbors who have "raged against them."

Isaiah → After Israel's reunification, they will defeat the Palestinians and the Jordanians

"He [God] will raise a banner for the nations and gather the exiles of Israel; he will assemble the scattered people of Judah from the four quarters of the earth . . . They [Israel] will swoop down on the slopes of Philistia to the west; together they will plunder the people to the east. They will subdue Edom and Moab, and the Ammonites will be subject to them."
–ISAIAH 11:12, 14 (EMPHASIS AND BRACKETS MINE)

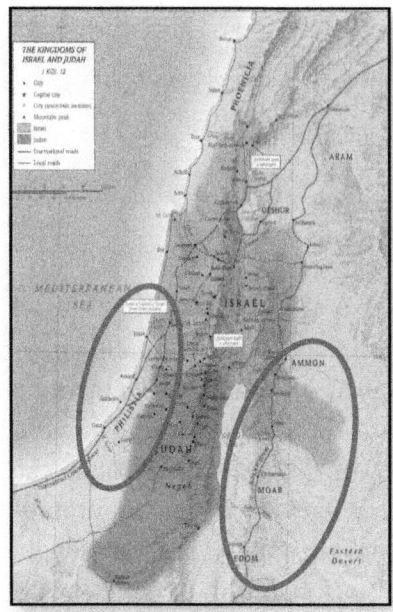

Above: The Kingdoms of Israel and Judah. Courtesy of Access Foundation. [Shapes mine]. Below: Photo © Pavalena. State of Israel. 2015. Istockphoto.com.[Shapes mine].

To the top left is a map of the Divided Kingdom of Israel and its neighbors, circa 900 B.C. Take note of the location of Philistia to the west of Israel and the locations of Ammon, Moab, and Edom to the east. These nations were a constant thorn in Israel's side over the early centuries of their existence. They often warred with one another.

It just so happened that in the 1967 Six Day War, Israel fulfilled this prophecy with their military might. Compare this modern lower map of that same region to the one above. During this war, Israel did in fact "swoop down" on Philistia (modern-day Gaza) and subdue them. Israel also subdued the Jordanians (once the ancient lands of Ammon, Moab, and Edom) and subjugated the Jordanian-controlled West Bank (an extension of Jordan near where Ammon existed), which is now being settled by Israelites. While Gaza and the West Bank have a de facto government called the Palestinian Authority (PA), they ultimately remain under Israeli control to this day.

The most important "plunder" that Israel took from Jordan was Jerusalem itself, and its holy sites there. We know this speaks of modern times because Isaiah says that this will happen after the Israelites return from their worldwide exile.

Micah→After the Israelites have returned to their land, they will crush Syria

"And he [the Messiah/the Lord] will be our peace when the Assyrian comes into our land, and when he treads in our palaces, then we will raise against him seven shepherds and eight princely men. They shall waste with the sword the land of Assyria and the land of Nimrod at its entrances; thus he shall deliver us from the Assyrian, when he comes into our land and when he treads within our borders."
–Micah 5:5-6 (KJV; EMPHASIS AND BRACKETS MINE)

To put this in context, we know this does not describe any conflicts with the ancient Assyrian Empire, because these events were to occur after the coming of the "ruler" from Bethlehem (a.k.a. Jesus). Verse 3 tells us that Israel will be abandoned for a time after his coming but that a remnant will one day return. It is after this return when this prophecy against Assyria and lands of Nimrod will take place (these locations indicate modern-day Syria).

The seven "shepherds" likely refer to modern Israel's defense minister (a shepherd is someone who protects), and the eight "princely men" implies the position of prime minister (a princely man, of course, is someone who rules). Since Israel has been reborn, four prime ministers (PMs) and three defense ministers have been in office that have gone to war with Syria. As we learned earlier, Syria tried to invade Israel in 1948, 1967, 1969, and 1973. Each time, Israel has repelled them, as this prophecy conveys. However, this prophecy also points to the fact that Israel will bring the fight to Syrian land to include the ancient lands of Nimrod (a renowned warrior from biblical antiquity who founded many cities in the Fertile Crescent region). During the Six Day War, Israel actually captured a Syrian-controlled region called the Golan Heights at its northern borders—it just so happens that the Nimrod Fortress National Park resides there. While the fortress which stands there now was built in the thirteenth century, it is suspected that Nimrod himself once had a fortress on the same mountain (Tourist Israel, "Nimrod Fortress"). Hence, the likely reason for its name.

This prophecy seems to indicate that Israel will have to deal with Syria several more times. It is clear, however, that while Israel was once dominated by the hordes of Assyria in ancient days, Israel now dominates them in conflict, as Micah foresaw.

Isaiah→Israel will bring terror to the Egyptians

> *"In that day, the <u>Egyptians will become weaklings</u>. They will shudder with fear at the uplifted hand that the Lord Almighty raises against them. And <u>the land of Judah will bring terror to the Egyptians</u>; everyone to whom Judah is mentioned will be terrified, because of what the Lord Almighty is planning against them."*
> –ISAIAH 19:16-17 (EMPHASIS MINE)

"In that day" refers to the context of the whole chapter, which is about the day of judgment against Egypt (which can mean a whole period of time, not just a literal day). While ancient Egypt had no fear of ancient Israel (back then, Egypt moved freely in Israel's lands), as we've already seen, the modern State of Israel has defeated Egypt four times in all out warfare. This prophecy seems to have in mind the Six Day War of 1967 in particular—Israel nearly obliterated Egypt's entire air force on the ground and overwhelmed their forces across the whole Sinai Peninsula in a matter of six days. Twice after, Egypt tried to reclaim their land from Israel and failed. Israel forced them to agree to a peace treaty in exchange for Sinai. It's safe to say that Egypt now has a healthy respect for Israel's military might.

Zechariah→After Judah is saved, Jerusalem will be an immoveable rock for the nations and Israel will defeat all nations around her

> *"I [the Lord] am going to <u>make Jerusalem a cup that sends all the surrounding peoples reeling</u>. Judah will be besieged as well as Jerusalem. On that day, when all the nations of the earth are gathered against her, <u>I will make Jerusalem an immovable rock for all the nations</u>. <u>All who try to move it will injure themselves</u> . . . On that day I will make the clans of Judah like a firepot in a woodpile, like a flaming torch among*

sheeaves. <u>They will consume all the surrounding peoples right and left</u>, but Jerusalem will remain intact in her place. <u>The Lord will save the dwellings of Judah first</u>, so that the honor of the house of David and of Jerusalem's inhabitants may not be greater than that of Judah."
—ZECHARIAH 12:2-7 (EMPHASIS MINE)

The Temple Mount. 2014. Jerusalem, Israel. Istockphoto.com.

These are bold words considering that when Zechariah prophesied this, Jerusalem was still a pile of rubble, courtesy of the Babylonians. The Jews rebuilt the city, but it was then destroyed by the Romans. In fact, Jerusalem has been fought over and changed hands many times over the centuries—certainly not the immovable rock of this prophecy . . . until the twentieth century.

Zechariah gives us a clue as to when this prophecy would "kick in"—sometime after the dwellings of Judah are saved, which will be before Jerusalem is saved. This is exactly the order of events since Israel was restored in 1948: The lands and homes of many of Israel's Jews (to include parts of ancient Judea) were spared in their war for independence against the Arabs, but Jerusalem remained mostly under Jordan's control. However, Israel reclaimed Jerusalem as their capital later, in 1967. First "Judah" was spared, then Jerusalem.

Since that day, the nations around Israel have tried to reclaim Jerusalem and been sent "reeling" each time, as this prophecy predicts.

The Muslims of the world, which now includes many nations, want Jerusalem back—the Palestinians claim it as their capital. But for now, they can't have it. Others want to see Israel totally obliterated, yet as we've seen, nobody else in their region has the strength to stand up to them. Israel has and continues to "consume all surrounding peoples" that try to attack her, but Jerusalem stays right where it should—in the hands of God's chosen nation. As we'll see in the next chapter, this prophecy will continue to be relevant until the nations of the world come together and seize Jerusalem one last time.

Ezekiel→Israel will become like the Garden of Eden

God speaking of future Israel:

> "The desolate land will be cultivated instead of lying desolate in the sight of all who pass through it. They will say, 'This land that was laid waste has become like the Garden of Eden; the cities that were lying in ruins, desolate and destroyed, are now fortified and inhabited.' Then the nations around you that remain will know that I the Lord have rebuilt what was destroyed and have replanted what was desolate. I the Lord have spoken, and I will do it."
> –EZEKIEL 36:34-36 (EMPHASIS MINE)

After the Roman invasions, the lands of Israel were pillaged and laid to waste. Josephus and Cassius Dio spoke of this in their accounts about the First and Second Jewish-Roman Wars. Notice that Cassius even implies that the Jews knew this would happen in advance (meaning through prophecy).

> "[N]early the whole of Judaea was made desolate, an event of which the people had had indications even before the war."
> –CASSIUS DIO, H.R., 5.69.14

Josephus reporting on the Roman siege of Jerusalem:

> "And now the Romans, although they were greatly distressed in getting together their materials, raised their banks in one and twenty days,

> *after they had cut down all the trees that were in the country that adjoined to the city, and that for ninety furlongs round about, as I have already related. And truly the very view itself of the country was a melancholy thing; for those places which were before adorned with trees and pleasant gardens were now become a desolate country in every way, and its trees were all cut down: nor could any foreigner that had formerly seen Judea and the most beautiful suburbs of the city, and now saw it as a desert, but lament and mourn sadly at so great a change: for the war had laid all the signs of beauty quite waste."*
> –JOSEPHUS, *W.J.*, 6.1.1 (EMPHASIS MINE)

The land remained desolate for centuries after war with the Romans. It was the ultimate judgment laid upon Israel as the Lord had promised through his prophets centuries before—its people purged and its land rendered little more than a desert. But, no more . . . since 1948, Israel has rapidly been fulfilling Ezekiel's prophecy about the land becoming a "Garden of Eden" and its ancient cities being rebuilt. The following prophecies provide us more detail of God's promises made to his people to restore their cities and land, and all find fulfillment in the modern State of Israel.

Isaiah→The Jews will rebuild their ancient cities

> *"Your [Israel's] people will rebuild the ancient ruins and will raise up the age-old foundations . . . They will rebuild the ancient ruins and restore the places long devastated; they will renew the ruined cities that have been devastated for generations."*
> –ISAIAH 58:12, 61:4 (BRACKETS MINE)

Not only did the prophets predict that the Jews would return to their land, but that they would rebuild over the ruins of their ancient cities destroyed by the Romans. Since the First Aliyah, Jews have been resettling ancient cities all across the lands of Israel. If we were to take out a modern map of Israel and start reading through the Bible, we would see the names of many cities out of antiquity inhabited once more.

The only other time Jews have returned to their land to rebuild was after the Babylonian exile, but that was only after a period of seventy years—hardly enough time to call their cities' ruins "ancient." No, here Isaiah was implying that after a very long time, his people would come to rebuild their nation—they have and continue to do so.

Isaiah→Foreigners will help rebuild Israel's cities and will work their lands and livestock

> *Isaiah continuing to speak of Israel's return:*
>
> *"Foreigners will rebuild your walls . . . "*
> —ISAIAH 60:10
>
> *"They will rebuild the ancient ruins . . . Strangers will shepherd your flocks; foreigners will work your fields and vineyards."*
> —ISAIAH 61:5

In the days of Israel's first return from exile, Arabs and other foreigners simply stood around harassing and threatening the Israelites as they rebuilt Jerusalem (Neh. 4), but since the rebirth of Israel in the twentieth century, it is a very different story. Arabs, along with many other Muslim and non-Muslim groups, lived in the land when Israel became independent once more. Over the last seven decades, these people have helped to rebuild all of Israel and tend to their resources. We can see the extent of this foreign help in our time: In 2012, 480,700 Arabs over the age of fifteen were counted among Israel's work force (Jerusalem Institute 2014, "Employment"). That's more than 15 percent of Israel's working population. Indeed, foreigners have been greatly involved in the restoration and reconstruction of Israel.

Isaiah→Reborn Israel will feed on the wealth of the nations and their leaders will serve them

Isaiah continuing to speak of Israel's future restoration:

> *"The wealth on the seas will be brought to you, to you the riches of the nations will come . . . and their kings will serve you . . . your gates will*

> *always stand open . . . so that people may bring you the wealth of*
> *the nations—their kings led in triumphal procession."*
> –ISAIAH 60:5B, 10-11
>
> *"You will feed on the wealth of nations,*
> *and in their riches you will boast."*
> –ISAIAH 61:6B

For such a small country, Israel continues to attract more attention on the world stage each passing year, and with that attention has come wealth. Whether it be tourism, trade, or financial support, Israel has been reeling in the "wealth of the nations" at an ever-increasing rate. In 2012, Israel hosted around 2,885,800 tourists from over 70 countries (CBS, "Tourist Arrivals"), who brought in over 4 billion dollars for Israel's economy. This is up from only 918 million in 2002—an increase of 438 percent! (CBS, "Tourism"). More and more come each year. Israel conducts trade with over 118 countries, which as of 2014 accounted for 63.5 billion dollars of income (CBS, "Trade Countries").

The second part of this prophecy is coming to be realized more and more as the world chooses sides with or against Israel. In recent years, many world leaders have personally engaged with Israeli leadership to show support and/or improve diplomatic or trade relations. Here are just a few:

President Barak Obama President George W. Bush.	United States	PM Shinzo Abe	Japan
President Vladimir Putin	Russia	Deputy PM Liy Yandong	China
PM David Cameron	Britain	President Luiz da Silva	Brazil
PM Stephen Harper	Canada	King Juan Carlos	Spain
President Francois Hollande President Nicolas Sarkozy	France	President Bronislaw Komorowski PM Donald Tush	Poland
President Joachim Gauck	Germany	PM Narendra Modi	India

President Giorgio Napolitano	Italy	President Martin Schulz	EU
PM George Papandreou	Greece	Secretary General Ban Ki Moon	UN

Most of these leaders have themselves travelled to Israel to conduct business in person. The rulers of the world are realizing Israel's potential and strategic value on many levels—as time goes on, many more will come to treat with them.

Not since Israel's glory days under King Solomon have they enjoyed such international recognition and support, and this prophecy was written long after that. Also, from that time until 1948, most kings who came to Israel were only interested in subjugating them or destroying them—they were not there to treat with them. Prophecies such as this were God's promise to return Israel to glory once more—we are witnessing this happen right now.

Isaiah→After Israel's people return, God will restore their desolate lands

> *"I [God] will make rivers flow on barren heights, and springs within the valleys. I will turn the desert into pools of water and the parched ground into springs. I will put in the desert the cedar and the acacia, the myrtle and the olive. I will set junipers in the wasteland, the fir and the cypress together, so that people may see and know, may consider and understand, that the hand of the Lord has done this, that the Holy One of Israel has created it."*
> −ISAIAH 41:18-20 (BRACKETS MINE)

For centuries since the devastation wrought by the Roman wars, Israel had been a relatively desolate place. Historians verify that this condition existed, and even grew worse up through the late nineteenth century:

In the twelve and a half centuries between the Arab conquest in the seventh century and the beginnings of the Jewish return in the 1880s, Palestine was laid waste. Its ancient canal and irrigation systems were destroyed and the wondrous fertility of which the Bible spoke vanished into desert and desolation . . . Under the Ottoman empire of the Turks, the policy of disfoliation continued; the hillsides were denuded of trees and the valleys robbed of their topsoil. (Voss 1953, 13)

We even have eyewitness reports from the hand of famous author Mark Twain, who visited the Holy Land in 1867:

Sometimes, in the glens, we came upon luxuriant orchards of figs, apricots, pomegranates, and such things, but oftener the scenery was rugged, mountainous, verdureless and forbidding . . . it [the Holy Land] truly is "monotonous and uninviting" . . . Of all the lands there are for dismal scenery, I think Palestine must be the prince. The hills are barren, they are dull of color . . . The valleys are unsightly deserts fringed with a feeble vegetation. . . It is a hopeless, dreary, heart-broken land . . . Palestine sits in sackcloth and ashes. (Twain 1869, 56)

Only fifteen years later, however, the Jews began to return with the First Aliyah, and the land began to see new life as they started to cultivate it once more. A British report to the League of Nations in 1921 outlines the rebirth of the land as the Jews finally start to return:

[T]he country [Palestine] was before the War, and is now, undeveloped and under-populated . . . The summits and slopes of the hills are admirably suited to the growth of trees, but there are **no forests** . . . The Jewish element of the population numbers 76,000 . . . . Prior to 1850 there were in the country only a handful of Jews . . . After the persecutions in Russia forty years ago, the movement of the Jews to Palestine assumed larger proportions. Jewish agricultural colonies were founded. They developed the culture of oranges and gave importance to the Jaffa orange trade. They cultivated the vine, and manufactured and exported wine. They drained swamps. They planted eucalyptus trees. They practised, with modern methods, all the processes of agriculture. There are at the present time 64 of these settlements, large and small . . . Every traveller in Palestine who visits them is impressed by the contrast between these pleasant villages, with the beautiful stretches of prosperous cultivation about them and the primitive conditions of life and work by which they are surrounded. (League 1921; emphasis mine)

For almost two thousand years, the inhabitants of Palestine could barely coax any food to grow in the land, but when the Jews returned, they were strangely blessed with a "green thumb." Or, perhaps, divinely blessed.

Since 1948, Isaiah's prophecy about the restoration of Israel's land has found total fulfillment. In making "rivers flow on barren heights," "Mekorot," Israel's national water company, has laid over twelve thousand kilometers of water pipelines across the country to carry water even into the Negev desert region. They have tapped the Sea of Galilee and numerous natural springs and underground reservoirs to distribute water everywhere in the country. Desalination facilities are bringing a growing supply of water to

Israeli drip irrigation system. Photo courtesy of Israel21c.org.

Israel from the Mediterranean. New reservoirs for this water across the country are turning "the desert into pools of water," and advanced irrigation systems are turning "parched ground into springs," which bring new life to Israel's land. From 1949 to 2011, the area of Israel's cultivated land grew from 637 to 1,583 square miles. Add in another 50 square miles worth of greenhouses by 2012 (Merkot 2014; Israel 2012, "Export").

All this access to water has allowed trees to grow across Israel once more. Since 1901, the Jewish National Fund (JNF) has been responsible for the planting of over 240 million trees, now covering more than 250,000 acres of land (JNF, "Forest & Ecology"). Where a century ago there were no forests, there are now 280-plus forests across the land of Israel (IMFA, "Conservation") in which now grow various cedars, acacias, cypress, pines, and a host of others. (KKL, JNF "Forests"). Olive, myrtle, and junipers are also found throughout the country now. Astonishingly, the JNF was able to get an entire pine forest to grow in the northern areas of the Negev Desert, known as the Yatir Forest, where the trees have adapted to survive (KKL, "Desert").

Mor, Benny. *Yatir Forest.* © Keren Kayemeth LeIsrael Jewish National Fund, Israel.

Through God's blessing, Israel has been able to restore its land and accomplish wondrous feats of agricultural engineering. They are bringing life to their land in a way their Arab neighbors could only dream of (just take a look at Google Earth). They have become almost self-sustaining regarding their food supply, and they export many of their agricultural goods and technologies all over the world. Their land has become amazingly fruitful once more, as Isaiah foretold. Take a look at the photos below to see just how much a "Garden of Eden" Israel has become

Photo courtesy of the University of Oregon Library. Mount Tabor, Israel, ca. 1915. Oregondigital.org.

Eli Zehavis. Mount Tabor. 2011.
http://www.pikiwiki.org.il.

over the last century.

War-ravaged heights such as Mount Tabor bear forests once more and provide views of lush farmland

The once desolate and foreboding Jezreel Valley is now green and cultivated.

Photo courtesy of the University of Oregon Library. Jezreel (Esdraelon) Valley ca. 1915. Oregondigital.org.

Jezreel Valley. 2014.

Numerous such water reservoirs now dot Israel's landscape, turning "the desert into pools of water and the parched ground into springs."

Above: Ron Mzr. Northern Israel. Accessed July 5, 2015.
www.publicdomainpictures.net.

Israel's once barren countryside is now filled with plentiful orchards of fruit. In fact, fruit is one of Israel's major exports.

©Kuna George. Accessed July 11, 2015. 123rf.com.

Micah→In the Last Days, people will stream to the Temple Mount

The Temple Mount in Jerusalem is quickly becoming the hottest piece of real estate on the planet. Jews, Muslims, and Christians all consider it sacred ground—which means a good majority of the world's population. Both of the Jewish temples to God were built here. The Western Wall stands as a testimony to the Second Temple it once enclosed. Jesus

> "In the last days the _mountain of the Lord's temple_ will be established as the highest of the mountains; it will be exalted above the hills, and peoples will stream to it . . ."
>
> –MICAH 4:1 (EMPHASIS MINE)

also walked these grounds, and many Muslims believe it is the site where Mohammed was taken bodily into heaven to visit Allah. Two mosques currently stand on the Mount, both considered highly sacred to Muslims.

The Temple Mount is highly valued for all these reasons, and so

with the capability of modern air travel, people of all faiths from all over the world are making pilgrimage to this holy site to come in contact with history and faith. In 2013, over 3.5 million tourists visited Israel, of which around 2.6 million spent time in Jerusalem (Reinstein 2014).

Around half a million non-Muslims are able to visit the site annually, but many more would visit if not for the long lines and security restrictions (Ronen 2014).

At the last height of Jerusalem's prosperity under Rome, the city was an important hub of commerce revolving around the Temple Mount, but it still only had religious value to a small percentage of the world's population at that time. Today, like no other time in history, the Temple Mount is highly valued by billions all over the world. The prophets knew this mount would become extremely important in "the Last Days." We are seeing this prophecy fulfilled now, with Israel opening up the floodgates of tourism to the world and by the Temple Mount's growing significance on the world stage. With the prevalence of Muslims among the nations, no other issue seems as likely to spark World War III as the growing Jewish threat to Muslim sovereignty over the Temple Mount. Its power to affect the world cannot be denied. It is truly becoming the most exalted and valued "mountain" on earth. But this is not the end of the prophecy . . .

> *"Many nations will come and say, 'Come, let us go up to the mountain of the Lord, to the temple of the God of Jacob . . .'"*
> –MICAH 4:2 (EMPHASIS MINE)

Photo by Juan R. Cuadra. Model of Herod's Temple. 1998. Holyland Model of Jerusalem. Museum of Jerusalem. Commons.wikimedia.org.

In the Last Days, a Third Temple of God will be built on the Temple Mount—just think of how many people will stream to it then! We know these two verses cannot be referencing the time of the Second Temple primarily because Micah 4:3 says that the Lord himself (Jesus) will teach and rule the nations from this temple—at which time there will be peace on Earth. (Obviously, this was not the case with either of the past temples, which were destroyed in the fires of war). A Third Temple must, therefore, be in Israel's future.

Make no mistake, it's not a matter of IF, but rather WHEN the new temple will be constructed. There are already organizations in place that are preparing for it and raising money for it. (Check out www.templeinstitute.org for more details.) It's already built on paper with fully modern design; all of the biblically mandated religious items have been remade to specs, including a recreation of the Ark of the Covenant— all of them on display at the Temple Institute. In March 2015, Jewish priests trained by the Institute's Cohanim Training Academy actually conducted a practice Passover sacrifice with live animals—the most accurate reenactment of Judaism's most important sacrifice since the Second Temple fell (Soffer 2015). The contingent of Jews wanting to see the Temple of God rebuilt is relatively small but growing. In 2013, a poll conducted by the Joint Forum of Temple Mount Organizations revealed that 30 percent of Jews are in favor of building a new temple on the Mount—to include 30 percent of secular Jews surveyed (Hasson 2013). The Temple Institute and other temple organizations are continuing to make progress in raising public awareness and appreciation for the importance of the temple and Torah (the Old Testament) in general. When the geopolitical climate is right, Israel will rebuild the temple once more. We will take another look at this prophecy and others regarding the Third Temple in the sections to come.

ISRAEL'S REBIRTH FORETOLD

Old Testament prophets predicted and historians affirm that

1. **Israel's national identity would remain in spite of being scattered across the globe** → Jews indeed retained their identity over two thousand years of being displaced without a home.

2. **After a worldwide exile, Jews would return to their Promised Land in 1948** → The days of Jews wandering the earth in payment of their sin ended in 1948, when Israel was restored as a sovereign nation.

3. **The nation of Israel would suddenly come into existence in a day and then come into strife** → Israel declared itself a sovereign nation and was immediately recognized by many other nations as such on May 14, 1948. She went to war for her independence the very next day.

4. **The tribes of Israel would once again be united and at peace with one another** → The State of Israel is a single, sovereign, democratic nation with a single ruler (the prime minister). Jews come to their homeland seeking to work together to rebuild what they have lost.

5. **Jews would return to Israel from their worldwide exile seeking God and Israel's ruler, David** → After Israel was reborn, many Jews sought to return to Israel in order to worship God freely and came home to their nation under the rule of a leader named David Ben-Gurion.

6. **After Israel's return from exile, God would put "shepherds" over them to help them and keep them from living in fear** → The United States has been a close ally of Israel since the beginning of its existence. Its support has been crucial for Israel's survival both economically and militarily. The US has nurtured Israel to the point that they are almost self-sustaining and can defend themselves from their enemies.

7. **The exiles of Israel would return to their home as doves through the clouds coming to nest** → Jews have been flying home to Israel in droves since 1948.

8. **Two nations to the north and south of Israel would resist allowing their Jews to return home** → Both the USSR and Ethiopia heavily restricted Jewish aliyah for years and required much persuasion to let them go.

9. **After return from exile, Israel would grow in strength and be empowered to destroy their enemies and make fools of them** → Israel has repelled every attack on their nation since day one and sent their invaders home in shame. They are quickly be-

coming a world military power and their technological advances in warfare are unmatched by most. Their society is also highly militarized. And, well . . . they've got nukes, so they aren't going anywhere.

10. **Israel would defeat the Palestinians and Jordanians and subjugate some of them** → Done in 1967 when Israel took Gaza and the West Bank.

11. **Israel would defeat Syria and take the battle to their land** → Israel has fended off Syria four times and taken the Golan Heights from them by force as a buffer zone.

12. **Israel would bring terror upon Egypt and make them look like weaklings** → Also done in 1967 when Israel obliterated Egypt's air force and overran their military in six days.

13. **After Jerusalem is saved for Israel, many nations will try to reclaim it and injure themselves** → Since Israel reclaimed Jerusalem in 1967, many have tried to take it back—all have failed miserably. Many still want to try—I think we know how that will turn out.

14. **After return from exile, the Jews will rebuild their ancient cities with the help of foreigners** → Many of Israel's ancient cities have been resurrected since 1948 and many non-Jews have greatly contributed to this effort.

15. **Reborn Israel will feed on the wealth of nations and their leaders will come to them** → Tourism and foreign aid bring mounds of money into Israel's economy from all over the world. Many world leaders, even in the last couple decades, have come to Israel to engage in diplomacy with them.

16. **Israel's long-desolate land will be restored to the point of springs, rivers, and trees in the desert** → Israel is turning more and more of its once barren landscape into a paradise, beautifully green and filled with agriculture, forests, and water.

17. **The nations will stream to the Temple Mount** → Christians, Jews, Muslims, and others from all over the world now pilgrim-

age to Jerusalem to walk on the holy mountain of God.

It has been over two thousand years since the OT was written, yet we see the words of the prophets—the Words of God—finding fulfillment on the pages of history to this day in a very specific and real way. With what we've seen of prophecy so far in this book, can anyone deny that there's something beyond our control going on here? The eerie accuracy of biblical prophecy time and again is too much to simply brush aside as mere coincidence. The implications of this cannot be ignored.

What all this means is that God's plan is marching forward. As we've seen in some of the Scriptures we have just read, with the rebirth of the nation of Israel, we are now in a period of history which the Bible refers to as "the Last Days" or "the Latter Days." Jerusalem has been reclaimed from the Gentiles by the Jewish people after almost two millennia. According to Jesus, this is a sign that the age of the Gentiles is coming to an end (Luke 21:24). These things imply that history as we know it is winding to a close—the final prophecies of Scripture are now on the horizon. Even if I weren't a Christian, it sure seems like this world is heading for a meltdown in a very bad way. Seemingly unstoppable evil is lurking everywhere on this planet—a cancer that cannot be cured through human force or reason. It is not just radical Islam which threatens the world, but a loss of rational thought, a loss of humanity, and a loss of wholesome values. Let's face it, this world is going crazy, and humans are not going to be able to fix it (aside from blowing ourselves up).

Does God's Word have the solution, then? If the Bible has been right so far, then what is yet to come? How does the story end? There is only one way the evil of this world can be brought to a stop and all wrongs be righted. There is only One who can finally bring peace and truth to this broken world. Who is this person and how does the story end? Let's find out.

The Era of the "Last" or "Latter Days"

This phrase, "the Last Days" or "the Latter Days" appears repeatedly in Scripture, especially prophetic Scripture. These phrases are the same in OT Hebrew and are used interchangeably. What are these Last Days, and when are they referring to? Most probably think of the End Times when hearing this phrase—a time close to the apocalypse and end of the world as we know it. While this is somewhat accurate, the Scriptures do not definitively provide a starting point to this last-days era, nor do all Hebrew uses of this phrase seem to point to the end of the world—context plays a big part in determining proper interpretation. Because of this, the Hebrew is sometimes translated as "in the days to come."

The writers of the New Testament (who wrote in Greek) spoke of the Last Days as well, but there is some debate as to when this era was to begin. Hebrews 1:2 and James 5:3 seem to indicate that "these last days" began sometime during Jesus' or the apostles' ministry on Earth—possibly after the Crucifixion, which ushered in the era of the New Covenant. In each of these cases, however, the context seems to imply that the writer was referring to events that have happened in "these recent days." On the other hand, 2 Timothy 3:1-7 and 2 Peter 3:3-4 speak of the depraved state of humanity that "will come" to be in the Last Days, implying that this era hadn't arrived yet. I will explore these passages in more detail in the coming chapters, but it is easy to see that humanity, on the whole, has been fulfilling these prophecies in a very literal way in recent decades. If we weren't in the "Last Days" during the apostles' time, we certainly are now.

This is reinforced by the OT prophecies, which we explored in this chapter—prophecies which mention their fulfillment in the Last Days, but that clearly had not been fulfilled until events of the twentieth century (Hos. 3:5 and Mic. 4:1). As we'll explore in the coming chapters, there are many more passages which refer to events yet to come in the Last Days, Latter Days, or time of "the end."

Whether the Last Days is a definitive period of time or simply indicative of future events, we are seeing prophecies regarding the Last Days or the Latter Days coming true within this last century. The simple fact that there are many more prophecies fulfilled now than are yet to come means that no matter how we look at it, we are approaching the final days before the coming of Christ (more on this shortly).

FROM HISTORY INTO ETERNITY

"Look, I am coming soon! My reward is with me, and I will give to each person according to what they have done. I am the Alpha and Omega, the First and the Last, the Beginning and the End."
—REVELATION 22:12-13

The Last Days are upon us. God has restored the nation of Israel as the prophets foretold, marking the transition to the final age of man and opening the door for the remaining prophecies of Scripture to become fulfilled. If you've stayed with me this far, I hope you can now see and appreciate God's hand on the Bible and on history—our existence truly is *his* story.

The Lord has been working since the beginning of time to bring about a people who would freely love him and obey him. Since the moment when man fell from God's grace, he has been working to bring us back to himself. God first revealed his plan to Abraham and through him brought about an entire nation whom he called his own. He brought them out of slavery, protected them, and gave them a home, yet in spite of all his blessings they would not accept him wholeheartedly and continued to break their covenant with him. Still, through this nation, God chose to send his Son, who would carry his name and his love, grace, and mercy to a sinful world that he might restore the relationship once lost. While many of the Gentiles began to accept Jesus, most of his own people still rejected him. And so, for this and their years of iniquity, God allowed them to be judged and scattered to the nations, while the Gentiles reaped the redemption and blessings brought through Jesus. But God did not forsake his people or his promises to them. He has returned Israel to center stage, and through them he will bring about the final act of his plan of judgment and redemption of this sinful world.

This final act is already written on the pages of God's Word, and if it has been right in predicting history so far, why shouldn't we believe it in foretelling these things to come? For if the coming prophecies are true, then they reveal serious implications for us all. I will do my best now to guide you through the major events yet to befall the human race in these Last Days.

OLD TESTAMENT TO NEW TESTAMENT PROPHECY

Before jumping right into apocalyptic prophecy, I first need to lay some groundwork. We are about to cross the bridge from Old Testament (OT) into New Testament (NT) prophecy, especially getting into the book of Revelation at the end of the Bible. There are some things we must consider and come to terms with before we can proceed.

The first question I would ask is, "How do we know NT prophecy is reliable and of God?" Couldn't it just be more hooey made up to scare people into belief? Let's explore these questions for a few moments. Chapters 2 through 4 proved that the OT prophets are reliable in their predictions of the future to include what they predicted about Jesus. Between the prophets and extra-biblical sources, it would appear that the gospel writers were telling the truth about the major facts surrounding Jesus' life and purpose. I also gave many other reasons in chapter 2 which support the trustworthiness of the Gospels. (If you still have doubts about this or the reliability of the rest of the NT Scriptures, please check out more literature on the subject by authors such as Josh McDowell, William Lane Craig, or Gary Habermas). The apostle John was one of the four gospel authors. If he was right about

Jesus, then we might want to heed the account of his vision of the distant future found in the book of Revelation. Most of the prophecies we will explore in the coming sections are found in this book.

One powerful testament to the reliability of the NT prophecies is that many of them find parallel support in the OT prophecies regarding the same people and events. Revelation is not the only book of the Bible to speak of apocalyptic prophecy—the OT is littered with it, as we'll soon discover. In light of this fact, contesting the NT writers on the truth of their prophecy would be somewhat irrelevant. This means, however, that NT prophets like John and Paul weren't making up their prophecies in order to scare people into belief—they were given wisdom to expound upon events that were already foretold. Besides, in both cases, their audience consisted of believers, as they were writing to various churches. If the OT prophets have been reliable so far, why shouldn't we believe that their prophecies will continue to come true? So, with the backing of the OT prophets, we will proceed to explore events to come. Time will ultimately prove whether the Old and New Testament prophets really did receive words from God on these matters.

Another issue to address is that of the supernatural. Much of what we are about to get into will be dealing with fantastic, supernatural events during which God will reveal himself to the world. Sure, it's one thing to believe it could have happened once upon a time, but wholly another thing to believe it will actually happen in the future in full view of everyone. But have we not just seen repeated evidence for the supernatural in the fulfillment of all the previous prophecies? God's hand is all over the Bible, and if so, then we are witnessing the supernatural every time prophecy is fulfilled.

In fact, the supernatural continues to happen all the time around the world, but many still want to deny it. I have been supernaturally healed of a heart condition and instantly cured of a shameful addiction. My wife has witnessed the exorcism of a demon-possessed child and an instant healing from blindness and lameness of a diabetic elderly woman. I also have a friend who has instantly healed people of sickness and broken bones. All these things were done by Jesus through the power of his name. It might take a lot to admit the supernatural does happen, but it does, it has, and will continue to do so. We should not be surprised, then, that the origin of all these supernatural things will show his power to all in days to come.

Interpretation of apocalyptic prophecy is also difficult compared to fulfilled prophecy for obvious reasons—it hasn't happened yet. As we've seen, prophecy is not always one continuous narrative but more like the assembling of a puzzle with different pieces of different issues coming from different prophets. In some cases the prophet might not have fully understood what he was seeing and described it in words that fit best for his time. The challenges I mentioned in chapter 1 regarding prophecy are compounded since these prophesied events haven't yet occurred—it's hard to know the proper way to interpret them and how to put the pieces together.

Revelation and other apocalyptic prophecies contain the full gambit of all these challenges: metaphors, symbolism, cyclic repetition, etc. To mitigate these issues, I have endeavored to make good use of context and compare/contrast NT and OT

Dating and Context of Revelation

There has been much speculation as to when the apostle John wrote this apocalyptic book. Some prophecy experts believe that John wrote this as a final warning to the Jews and Christians about the Great Tribulation of 70 A.D., but I believe he was mostly speaking of future events for several reasons:

1. While Revelation mentions seeing the souls of the survivors of the Great Tribulation early on (Rev. 7:9-17), John goes on to describe many future events in the book, most of which do not appear to have happened yet, and barely any of which have any resemblance to the events of the Jewish-Roman war.

2. Revelation describes Jesus coming again to save Israel and bring justice to the nations and people of Earth. In 70 A.D., it was Israel whom God was judging.

3. Church father Irenaeus, disciple of Polycarp, who was a direct disciple of John, dated the writing of Revelation near the end of Caesar Domitian's reign (81–96 A.D.). This means John's vision was of events well after 70 A.D., and Irenaeus referred to them as such (Irenaeus, *A.H.* 5.30.3). Who better to understand John's writing than a man who knew John's understudy!

Scriptures to get to the truth behind each prophecy and pull the pieces together in a way that makes sense and that I can justify.

I will not pretend to know the exact timing of these events, only the approximate order in which they will occur. These prophecies are there to act as markers on the road to the coming of Christ's kingdom on Earth. They function more as an hourglass running down to this event rather than a stopwatch. As each prophecy is fulfilled, we can see that the hourglass loses a little more sand and the final events are getting closer, but we don't know the exact amount of time left in the sand before it's gone. Jesus himself said that only God the Father knows the exact timing of Jesus' return (Matt. 24:36). It is my point in this chapter to merely reveal the major events that are yet to come along the road to the coming of this kingdom so that you can make some informed decisions about what all this means for your life.

DRAMATIS PERSONAE

It will be immensely helpful in our prophetic reading to identify the main players involved and the various titles that the OT/NT writers use in referencing them:

JESUS = God, The Lord, the Lamb, the Holy One, Christ, Faithful and True, the Word of God, King of kings, Lord of lords, Prince of princes, Messiah, The Ancient of Days, The Most High.

SATAN = The Devil, the Dragon, the ancient serpent.

THE ANTICHRIST = The Beast, the lawless or sinful one, the little horn, the King Who Exalts Himself; Gog. He will be a world leader who will arise near the time of Christ's return to deceive, rule, and oppress the people of Earth.

THE FALSE PROPHET = The second beast. A religious leader who will endorse the Antichrist and perform signs and wonders in his name. This false prophet will create an image of the Beast and force the people of Earth to worship it.

THE TWO WITNESSES = The two olive trees; the two lampstands. They are two prophets of God who will appear in Jerusalem after its fall to the Beast. They will prophesy about things to come and bring down plagues of judgment upon the Beast and his worldwide kingdom for 3.5 years.

THE ANGEL OF THE ABYSS = "The beast that comes up from the Abyss." Some theologians believe this to be a demon unleashed to terrorize our world during the End Times.

VISIONS OF THINGS TO COME

The best way to understand and present God's final plans is to lay out this story in plain English, combining all the Scriptures involved into a coherent narrative. There are many apocalyptic Scriptures which interweave and share details of the same events, so I will simply cite them together instead of writing them all out individually. This narrative will allow us to take a look at the "box top" of this apocalyptic puzzle before examining how and why the pieces go together. For those who wish to do so, the appendix will break down each part of the narrative to do just that. Please keep in mind that this is my personal interpretation after much study and cross-referencing of Scripture and commentaries, but neither I nor any other authority on prophetic Scripture (except God) will ever have the 100 percent correct interpretation. The main themes and ideas, however, are obvious and should not be ignored. I will attempt to justify some of my below interpretations in the appendix. For now, let's begin with prophecies of present day, and then move forward into eternity . . .

In these Last Days, the people of Earth will become increasingly selfish and evil. They will be lovers of material things and pleasure than of God, hateful and brutal towards one another, and will display false spirituality and godliness. They will continue to learn and believe new ideas, but will never really come to knowledge of the truth (2 Tim. 3:1-9).

They will scoff at Christians, saying, "Where is this great 'coming' which Jesus promised?" while denying that this same Jesus was the one who created the heavens and earth and forgetting that he destroyed the world's evil once before in the Great Flood. However, it is not God's sole desire to destroy mankind but to save as many as possible—those who will come to repentance of their sinful lives and accept his Son. So, he is patient in carrying out the last stage of his plan (2 Pet. 3:3-9). Before the end, God will ensure that the Gospel of Salvation through Jesus reaches all corners of the earth (Acts 1:8). Even now, Jesus' many disciples are bringing his message of love to the darkest of places in this world.

Meanwhile, God has been revealing his wrath and judgment upon Earth—turning up the pressure year by year. God has unleashed the "Four Horsemen" into the world, who bring forth natural disasters, take peace from the earth, sow desire for war, and cause men to kill one another (Rev. 6:1-8). The number and ferocity of natural disasters is rising: famine, plague, earthquakes, and tsunamis. So, too, is the increase in number of conflicts, persecutions, and impending strife. Eventually, even the cosmos will begin to rain death and destruction upon our planet (Rev. 8).

Center: Doré, Gustave. The Vision of Death. Ca 1875. www.wikiart.org. Top Right: ©Igor Zhuravlov. Accessed July 11, 2015. 123rf.com. Bottom Right: ©Tomas Griger. Accessed July 11, 2015. 123rf.com.

As these things come to pass, the nation of Israel will ever-increasingly become the center of the world's attention. One day, they will finally be able to rebuild the Temple of the Lord in Jerusalem (Isa. 60:13; Mic. 4:1-3), either through force of Zionism or by allowance of the nations. However, there will not be room enough for its original outer courts due to the "Gentile" hold on part of the Mount (Rev. 11:1-2).

During these dark days, sometime after the temple is built, a league of ten nations will come together and give power to a dark and sinister leader known as "the Beast," who is also called the Antichrist. Satan will bestow upon this man great power and authority over the world. He will speak out against the Lord and the people of Israel, taunting and blaspheming them (Dan. 7:23-25; Rev. 13:1-8, 17:12-13). He will be fatally wounded, but when he survives, the world will be in awe of him, follow him, and worship him . . . except for those who follow Jesus (Rev. 13:3-4, 8). The Beast will then exalt himself above all other gods and seek to magnify his power and glory in the world (Dan. 11:36-37; 2 Thess. 2:4a). A second "beast," known as the "False Prophet," will rise and aid him in this goal by performing supernatural signs of power to deceive the nations as to the Beast's divinity. This prophet will force the world to worship the Beast and his false image and to receive a mark of allegiance to him. Those who refuse will be killed (2 Thess. 2:9-10; Rev. 13:11-17).

The Beast will then bring the nations to wage war on the people of Israel. They will defeat God's Holy People and Jerusalem will be conquered. The city will be plundered and its women raped. It will be delivered into the Beast's hands for three and a half years and half of the city's people will be exiled (Dan. 7:25, 8:24, 11:41; Zech. 14:1-3; Rev. 11:2, 13:7). The Beast will then establish his rule from the Lord's Temple, where he will sit and proclaim himself to be God (Dan. 11:45; 2 Thess. 2:4).

During this same time, two prophets (the Two Witnesses) will stand up in the captured city of Jerusalem. Empowered by God, they will call forth plagues of judgment upon the earth, and anyone who tries to kill them will be destroyed. Festering sores will break out on all people who have accepted the mark of the Beast and worshipped its image. The seas, springs, and rivers of the earth will be turned to blood, killing all that is in them. The sun will flare up and scorch the earth and its inhabitants, but they will curse God's name and refuse to repent of their sin and honor him. Then the Beast's worldwide kingdom will be plunged into darkness—the people will sit in agony suffering from their sores (Rev. 11:3-6, 16:1-11).

At the end of these three and a half years of torment, the Angel of the Abyss will be allowed to kill the Two Prophets who wrought so much destruction and suffering, but ultimately for God's glory. The whole world will gloat over their carcasses and celebrate, but after three and a half days, God will bring them back to life and call them into heaven, leaving the world in shock (Rev. 11:7-12).

The Beast will see that the people of Israel have been recovering from the previous war and that they have been living in safety and health from the plagues brought forth on the earth (Ezek. 38:1-9,14; Dan. 8:25). He will rage against them and once more reach out to the nations to bring an army down upon Israel like none other before assembled. Armies from nations such as Russia, Iran, Libya, Sudan, Ethiopia, Turkey, and many others will descend upon Israel in a great horde covering the land (Ezek. 38:1-16; Dan. 7:21; Joel 3; Rev. 16:14). They will clash with the hopelessly outnumbered forces of Israel in a place called Har Megiddo (a.k.a. Armageddon, the Jezreel Valley, or Valley of Jehosaphat), which is northwest of Jerusalem (Joel 3:2, 12; Rev. 16:16). It is there, in that wide open stretch of land, where the fate of the world will be decided.

Jezreel Valley near the ancient city of Megiddo, Israel.

What happens next will be a day unlike any in the history of mankind—the great day of God's wrath (Isa. 13:9, 34:8; Ezek. 38:18-19; Rev. 16:19b). The armies of the Beast will destroy much of Israel's forces (Dan. 7:21, 8:25b) and will advance across all the mountains of Israel. When all seems lost, a great earthquake will shake the entire world. Mountains and cities will crumble, and all people will tremble at the presence of the Lord. Jerusalem will split apart, as will the Mount of Olives to its east (Ezek. 38:19-20; Zech. 14:4; Rev. 6:12-17, 16:18-19). The sun, moon, and sky will go dark (Joel 3:15; Rev. 6:12).

©Igor Zhuravlov. Accessed July 11, 2015. 123rf.com

And then, coming with the sound of trumpets, Jesus—the Son of Man, the Lamb of God, the Ancient of Days—will descend from the clouds in great power and glory. All the earth will mourn when they look upon him and realize the truth—that there is only one God, and he has come to bring judgment upon the sinful nations of man. Israel, too, will mourn when they realize that this Jesus is indeed their Messiah and that they had crucified him at the time of his first coming (Dan. 7:22; Zech. 12:10; Matt. 24:30; Rev. 14:14). But those who already called Jesus their Savior, his elect, will in that moment be gathered to heaven from all over the world to meet him in the clouds—first those believers who had died for not worshipping the Beast, and then those who remained in the world (Matt. 24:31, 36-41; 1 Thess. 4:16-17; 2 Thess. 2:1; Rev. 14:15-16, Rev. 20:4). Jesus' elect will then be spared from what is left to come upon the world, but Jesus will then move to save Israel.

The armies that stand against Israel and the Lamb will turn on one another. Rain, massive hailstones, and fire will fall upon them and across the entire planet. There will be no question that God has arrived (Ezek. 38:21-23; Zech. 14:13; Rev. 16:21). Between the earth-quake and the falling sky, people all over the world will hide from the Lamb, knowing that the day of his wrath has come (Rev. 6:15-17). As Jesus provides a way for the people of Israel to flee the battle, he will come with the multitudes of heaven and the remaining soldiers of Israel and lay waste to the armies of the earth assembled against them. The Beast will then be destroyed and cast into the Lake of Fire (Isa. 66:15-16; Ezek. 39:3-5; Dan. 7:11, 26, 8:25; Zech. 14:3-5; Joel 3:11-13; 2 Thess. 2:8; Rev. 19:11-21). The slaughtered dead will be so great around Jerusalem that the blood will cover the land up to six feet deep for 180 miles (Rev. 14:19-20). Afterward, all of the nations who fought against Jerusalem will be struck with a horrific plague in return for their wickedness—man and beast alike will perish (Zech. 14:12, 15). The kingdoms of the Beast will fall and his reign will finally be over . . . the reign of Jesus will then begin.

Those of Israel's enemies who survive this great battle will return to the distant lands from which they came and proclaim God's glory to those that remain in the world—their eyes finally open to the truth (Isa. 66:19). Meanwhile, Satan will be banished for a thousand years (or, at least, a very, very long time), so that he will be unable to lead men astray (Rev. 20:1-3). Then, Christ will establish his millennial kingdom on Earth, and those believers who were brought up to him on the Day of Wrath will reign with him over the rest of the earth during this period (Dan. 7:27; Rev. 20:4-5). Jesus will take up his rule in the temple on Mount Zion. From here, his law will go out into the world, and he will settle any disputes among the people or the na-tions. Peace will reign (Mic. 4:2b-3). The survivors of the nations will come to see the Lord on his throne, to worship, to bring tribute, and to learn knowledge and wisdom from him. Those nations that do not go to pay tribute to the Lord or celebrate the Feast of Tabernacles will be punished (Isa. 66:20; Mic. 4:2; Zech. 14:16-19). These will be the last days for the non-believers of earth to accept Jesus as their Lord. However, not everyone will.

At the end of this millennium, after the earth has recovered from God's wrath and repopulated, Satan will be allowed into the world one last time to deceive many and weed out those who are not faithful to the Lord. He will take as many people down with him as he can. He will raise a massive army from all the nations once more and bring it against Jerusalem. This time, however, there will be no fighting against the Lord. He will consume the armies of the world with fire, and Satan will be thrown into the Lake of Fire to join the Beast and his prophet (Rev. 20:7-10).

Doré, Gustave. *The Last Judgment*. Ca. 1875. www.wikiart.org.

After this, all the remaining dead of the earth will be called before the throne of Jesus in all his glory. Then they will be judged according to their deeds in life. Those whose names are not written in the Book of Life will be cast from God's presence into the Lake of Fire, the second death. This will include "the cowardly, the unbelieving, the vile, the murderers, the sexually immoral, those who practice magic arts, the idolaters, and all the liars." Those whose names are in the Book will partake in everlasting life with the Lord and all who follow him (Dan. 12:1-2; Matt. 25:31-46; John 6:39-40, 12:48; 2 Thess. 1:6-10; Rev. 20:11-15; 21:8).

Then, the Lord Jesus will declare that he is making everything new. The old heaven and earth will pass away in fire, and a new heaven and earth will come to be. God will set a new Jerusalem on

Doré, Gustave. *The New Jerusalem*. Ca. 1875. www.wikiart.org.

Earth as his holy city. It will be the inheritance of all who have accepted Jesus as Lord and Savior. They will drink from the waters of eternal life, and the Lord will live among them and be their light. There will be no more death or mourning or crying or pain. All those who follow the Lord and his ways will be with him and reign with him for all eternity (Isa. 66:22; 2 Pet. 3:7, 10, 13; Rev. 21, 22).

And so, this is how the story ends—with the destruction of evil, the restoration of a fallen world, and the redemption of man into the presence of God for all who call Jesus Lord and Savior. Let no one say, after reading this, that God does not do anything about evil in this world! He will most certainly settle all accounts by the end for those who have not been forgiven through Jesus. The God of the universe is indeed wholly good and wholly just in his final plan for humanity—a good God cannot allow sin to go unpunished. The end of sinful man might seem brutal, but God has no tolerance for sin, and he will purge it from the earth like a cancer.

But he also has amazing things in store for those who decide to follow and worship him. Imagine a world where all citizens follow one perfect king, and everyone follows his perfect way of living—not just because they must, but because they have chosen to. No one will have need to lie or steal or fight or murder, as we will have everything we could possibly need provided for us. Death and hunger and pain will be a fleeting memory. We will all have Jesus in common and live to worship him and enjoy eternity with him and with one another in harmony. It will be the end of one story and the beginning of a whole new one, the likes of which we cannot truly imagine.

THE MEANING OF THINGS TO COME

Now that we have seen the "box top," what does all this mean for each of us? The apostle Peter put it well:

> "Since everything will be destroyed in this way, what kind of people ought you be? You ought to live holy and godly lives as you look forward to the day of God and speed its coming. That day will bring

> *about the destruction of the heavens by fire, and the elements will melt in the heat. But in keeping with his promise we are looking forward to a new heaven and a new earth, where righteousness dwells. So then, dear friends, since you are looking forward to this, make every effort to be found spotless, blameless and at peace with him . . . since you have been forewarned, be on your guard so that you may not be carried away by the error of the lawless and fall from your secure position. But grow in the grace and knowledge of our Lord and Savior Jesus Christ . . ."*
> —2 PETER 3:11-14,17-18

Whether you currently accept Jesus as your Savior or don't, these verses apply to all. We have all been warned of what is to come. Our only salvation is Jesus himself. I know which side of that final battle I want to be on. We should all be seeking Jesus' grace and to better walk in his footsteps.

If I only had the book of Revelation by itself, I might find it all a little too fantastic . . . a little too outlandish. But, as we can see, Revelation finds support throughout the entire Old and New Testaments. I think we've established that the OT prophets certainly knew what they were talking about when they spoke of the future. They saw many of the same events that John witnessed in his vision. If the prophets were right about Jesus, were right about the fall of Jerusalem, and were right about the restoration of Israel (along with many other things throughout history), why then should we doubt what they have to say about the End Times?

If they are right, and it appears that they will be, then what we have just studied holds serious implications not just for our lives here on Earth but also for our eternal souls. Those who don't have Jesus are risking serious consequences if these things are true. If nothing else at this point, wouldn't it seem prudent to at least investigate further into the truth of God's Word than scoff at it or turn a blind eye? You have only everything to gain in accepting the love, grace, salvation, and eternal life offered through Jesus Christ.

FINAL CONCLUSIONS

We have journeyed through prophecy and history and even glimpsed into the future to see the last chapter of mankind on this earth. Now, let's bring everything together and see the full picture and meaning of all that we have covered:

> **1. We've explored 52 prophecies, which we know were written no later than 100 B.C., and which were specifically fulfilled in history thereafter.**

> ➤ And there are many more we could discuss, especially if we can agree that the OT was completed in the 400s B.C., much earlier.

> **2. Only a divine hand could ensure all these things came true over the span of two thousand years.**

> ➤ How many fulfilled, specific prophecies does it take before we can believe divine intervention in the writing of the books of the Bible? A few of these prophecies might have come true on a guess, but all of them? Not a chance, especially when some predicted events accurately, right down to the year and month!

> ➤ If one is to deny a divine hand on the Bible, he or she must somehow be able to explain away each and every one of these prophecies by natural means (and there are many more than this). To claim blind luck would take more faith than admitting the truth.

> **3. God's hand is on the Bible and all of history.**

> ➤ Prophecy is God's fingerprints on the Bible. It is how we can know that it is from him, as no one else can claim the amount or accuracy of such prophecy. God in fact challenges the other religions of the world to match the prophecy-driven truth of his Word:

> *"'Which of their gods foretold this [the Jews' return from worldwide exile] and proclaimed to us the former things? Let them bring in their*

witnesses to prove they were right, so that others may hear and say,
'It is true.' 'You are my witnesses,' declares the Lord, 'and understand
that I am he. Before me no god was formed, nor will there be one after
me. I, even I, am the Lord, and apart from me there is no savior.
I have revealed and saved and proclaimed—I, and not some foreign
god among you. You are my witnesses,' declares the Lord, 'that I am
God. Yes, and from the ancient of days I am He. No one can deliver
out of my hand. When I act, who can reverse it?'"
–Isaiah 43:9-13 (brackets mine)

➢ The prophecies of the Bible are tied to reality more so than any other religion can claim—we just learned to what extent this is so: to the point of predicting history before it happened time and time again in very specific ways.

➢ Through this prophecy, God asserts that he is Lord and Savior alone, and that he is in control—God has a plan that won't be stopped. After all that we have explored, can we deny this? Whatever the prophets have said always comes to reality—I have yet to encounter prophecy that hasn't come true in its expected time. Every time I have seen attempts to show prophecy failed, it was a case of either not considering the context/timing of a prophecy's occurrence, of bad interpretation, or of claims unsupported by good research. (More on this in appendix 2.)

4. If the Bible is of God, then it must be true.

➢ This is a self-evident conclusion—when God speaks, then whatever he says must be truth. It would be quite hypocritical of God to proclaim lying as evil while doing it himself. Besides, what reason would an all-knowing, all-powerful God have to lie when he's made it clear that he wants an open, honest, loving relationship with us, his children? Therefore, we can know that the Bible is truth.

➢ Anything that contradicts God's truth is by default false, no matter what we may choose to believe.

> If Jesus really was whom the prophecies foretold, the Gospels proclaim, and secular history supports, then it's not a matter of just religion and faith, but of HISTORY. Our beliefs, then, can't change the historical fact that God walked this earth in the flesh and came to die as the ONLY salvation for our sins. Why would he have gone through all this if there were other options available?

5. If the Bible is true, and was right in its predictions of all these historical events, then what it says about future events is true as well.

> The Bible predicts that one day Jesus will return to bring all his followers to himself and to destroy evil and cast out all who have rejected him.

6. We all have a serious choice to make.

I hope you have enjoyed this journey through prophecy and history and have come away with an appreciation for the power and relevance of God's Word and its truth. If you are already a follower of Jesus, it is my hope that this book will both encourage you in your faith and imbue you with a sense of urgency and purpose to serve God's kingdom with whatever gifts he has given you. Jesus is going to return, and he expects to find his followers to be doing his work and will reward them accordingly (Matt. 24:45-51, 25:14-28). If you have not yet invited Jesus into your life, he is still knocking on your door. He wants more than anything to have your heart and bring you to himself, but he will not break the lock and charge on in—only you can let him in. When you do, you will get to experience his love, his forgiveness, his grace, and a peace that passes all understanding.

When we stand before the Lord one day, all who have accepted Jesus will have their name written in the Book of Life. And when God sees our name in the Book and Jesus in our hearts, instead of condemning us for our sin, he will simply say, "You are forgiven." Then we will get to join in a vast community of Christ-followers from every tribe, tongue, and nation, living at peace with one another under the awesome love of our creator.

While some might still be appalled at the fate which befalls those who do not accept Jesus, let us not forget that God takes sin seriously enough to have come down here, suffer a brutal death on a Roman cross, and experience his own judgment so that we might not have to. He loves us THAT much! What other god known to man has done something like this? What other god has lowered himself to our level that he might serve us, experience what we go through in life, and suffer as we do? What other god is more worthy to cast judgment than the only God who lived the perfect life that we could not and still paid the ultimate penalty in our place? Rest assured that in the end, all things will be fair and all accounts settled through the wisdom of Christ.

If you are still struggling to believe after all that we've revealed about God's Word, then I encourage you to continue to explore for the truth—there is so much evidence for the truth of the Bible out there besides even prophecy. I realize that this book does not answer all difficulties and questions surrounding the Bible—Scripture can be complicated. But I hope I've been able to show through prophecy that it is of God, it is trustworthy, and it is true. We should give it the benefit of the doubt in exploring other tough issues.

If you think all this is a bunch of malarkey and don't desire to delve any further, then I encourage you to be open and honest with yourself in seeking the truth and to challenge your beliefs if you never have—test them. I encourage you to ask yourself: "Are my religious beliefs driven by verifiable truth? Or are my beliefs driven by what I want to be true or by what I have grown up believing?" I posed these questions to myself, and I would pose them to anybody. In the end, the truth won me over, and my faith is stronger than ever. If nothing else, I encourage you to stay in the news, especially regarding Israel. As you see the events of this chapter unfolding, I pray you will think back to this book and reconsider the truth and salvation of Jesus Christ before it's too late.

The choice to follow Jesus is not one to be taken lightly, either way

(Jesus did not guarantee his followers a strife-free life on this earth—quite the opposite in fact), but I think we can all agree that if God's Word is true, then this choice will be one which will affect us for all eternity. After all we've learned, it certainly appears to be true—is it worth the risk to ignore? Or is it a much better notion to answer the knock at your heart's door and let Jesus come in and be a part of your life? Will you say "no" to the things that keep you from a relationship with your heavenly Father, lay all your hurts and regrets at Jesus' feet, and say "yes" to his gift of grace and forgiveness? It is my prayer and my hope that you will, for he is seeking you with all his heart and has more love for you than you could possibly imagine. God bless you.

"HERE I AM! I STAND AT THE DOOR AND KNOCK. IF ANYONE HEARS MY VOICE AND OPENS THE DOOR, I WILL COME IN AND EAT WITH THAT PERSON, AND THEY WITH ME."
—REVELATION 3:20

For those that want to explore deeper into the prophecies of this chapter and why I interpreted them as I did, I encourage you to read on!

APPENDIX 1: PUTTING THE PIECES TOGETHER

For those of you who are interested in seeing how the pieces of the End Times puzzle fit together or are wondering why I interpreted some of the predicted events a certain way, this section provides my in-depth interpretations and justifications for them. I left this section out of the main body of text so as not to bog down the narrative and take away from its contribution to the conclusion of the book. Seeing as how entire books can be written on such prophecy, I simply focus on the main ideas and most controversial interpretations amongst biblical scholars.

Now let's rewind back to the beginning of this final chapter of Earth's history and take a closer look at the prophecies themselves. Again, I will cite the many Scripture references which accompany the narrative, but I will not directly quote most of them, as I would be quoting entire chapters of Scripture in some cases. I highly encourage you to read through the Scripture references, however, as it will greatly enhance your understanding of the narrative and how everything fits together.

THE CONDITION OF MAN

All these things are true of the direction mankind is going. In this last century, we have witnessed the most horrific evils known to mankind: wars, genocides, and persecutions that have ended millions upon

> *"In these last days, the people of Earth will become increasingly selfish and evil, lovers of material things and pleasure than of God, hateful and brutal towards one another, and will display false spirituality and godliness. They will continue to learn and believe new ideas, but will never really come to knowledge of the truth."*
> –2 Tim. 3:1-9

189

millions of lives; weapons of terrifying mass destructive power; and the hateful brutality of radical Islam, modern dictators, and renegade groups vying for power.

Just looking at our own nation, we have become exceedingly self-ish, materialistic, and pleasure-seeking. The mindset of entitlement is running rampant in our society—everybody gets a "gold star" or a free handout—much complaining occurs if they don't. We are increasingly bombarded with advertising and scurry around to get the best deals on meaningless stuff. We worship people who can entertain us best or women who have no other skill in life than looking hot and spending the money we hand over to them. Meanwhile, American soldiers get paid a pittance to go sacrifice their lives so that we are safe and free to blow all our money on these and other mindless pleasures. Our nation is backwards in its priorities and values, as are many others around the world.

Regarding the spiritual aspect, the number of people in the US who consider themselves "spiritual but not religious" is on the rise, especially in younger generations. One study shows that as of 2012, around 20 percent of our population consider themselves religiously "unaffiliated," but most still consider themselves spiritual (Pew 2012). More and more people come to proclaim a sense of spirituality or false godliness while denying the truth behind it (2 Tim. 3:5).

Our decline in wholesome, widely-accepted values is due in part to the growing idea of relativism and pluralism—the idea that we all are entitled (did I say entitled again?) to our own values and religious beliefs, and that somehow everybody can be right, but nobody can be wrong. (Unless you voice Christian beliefs that conflict with someone else's values.) As our society slides away from a central standard of beliefs and values (which was once the Bible), of course we are going to see an increase in self-centered thinking—because religion and spirituality is now all about me and what I want! And so, many do go about with many new ideas about spirituality, but never come to knowledge or admittance of the truth of Jesus and the Bible.

SCOFFERS, NAYSAYERS, AND GOD'S DESIRE TO SAVE MANY

They will scoff at Christians saying, "Where is this great 'coming' which Jesus promised?" while denying that this same Jesus was the one who created the heavens and earth and forgetting that he destroyed the world's evil once before in the Great Flood. However, it is not God's sole desire to destroy mankind but to save as many as possible—those who will come to repentance of their sinful lives and accept his Son. So, he is patient in carrying out the last stage of his plan (2 Pet. 3:3-9). Before the end, God will ensure that the Gospel of Salvation through Jesus reaches all corners of the earth (Acts 1:8). Even now, Jesus' many disciples are bringing his message of love to the darkest of places in this world.

Peter definitely foresaw the changing of the times—where Christianity in Western culture is now being more and more ridiculed and mocked. The "New Atheist" movement has been attacking Christianity left and right, and our kids who claim Christianity are increasingly laughed at in grade school and college, where fifty years ago, Christianity was the norm. The fact that Jesus promised to return, yet hasn't after two-thousand-plus years, has definitely brought much scoffing and nay-saying against Christianity.

There is a reason that Jesus has not yet returned. We must realize that God is delaying his second coming because he wants to bring peoples from every tribe and nation to himself (Rev. 7:9). He wants his name and his glory to be taken to all parts of the earth. While there are still thousands of unreached people groups or ethnicities in the world, Christianity is rapidly reaching into the darkest areas of our planet to include Africa (where Pentacostalism is exploding), India, Afghanistan, Iran, and even North Korea. At great risk to their own lives, Christian missionaries are carrying the hope and love of Jesus to a world that desperately needs him.

Yep, we're still waiting for the Second Coming. But as I see prophecy continue to unfold, I know it's getting closer. I am therefore encouraged and entirely justified in my beliefs and patience. People may scoff at us all they want, but this is why we wait . . . this is why we are patient and diligent to see God's plan fulfilled. This is why I am writing this book.

GOD'S INCREASING WRATH AND JUDGMENT

Meanwhile, God has been revealing his wrath and judgment upon Earth—turning up the pressure year by year. God has unleashed the "Four Horsemen" into the world, who bring forth natural disasters, take peace from the earth, sow desire for war, and cause men to kill one another (Rev. 6:1-8). The number and ferocity of natural disasters is rising: famine, plague, earthquakes, and tsunamis. So, too, is the increase in number of conflicts, persecutions, and impending strife. Eventually, even the cosmos will begin to rain death and destruction upon our planet (Rev. 8).

These horsemen are likely just a metaphor, but what they represent is most certainly not. While it's hard to say just how long the "Four Horsemen" have been at work in the world, one thing is certain—their efforts have become increasingly effective. This last century has certainly lived up to the prophecy.

The "white horse" was to sow the desire for conquest all over the world. The twentieth and twenty-first centuries have had no shortage of men bent on conquest, which led to the two largest wars in history, countless countries and factions warring with one another for power, and a cold war which almost blew up the entire planet. Now we have ever-increasing numbers of radical Islamist groups bent on taking over the world and Russia making land grabs again.

On similar grounds, the "red horse" was to go throughout the earth taking away peace and making men kill each other. Africa and the Middle East especially have been suffering from this curse. The Arab Spring of 2011 suddenly brought much conflict and killing to the Middle East, which then gave birth to the brutal Islamic State movement. Thanks to the likes of Hamas, Islamic State, Al Qaeda, and others, Muslims are attacking Jews and anyone else they don't like at random, all over the world. How long before Westerners start regularly attacking Muslims out of fear and revenge? Any time spent in the news, and one can see how much mindless killing and lack of value for life there is in this world. We seem to be stuck in a downward spiral of "You kill my people, I kill yours."

The "black horse" and the "pale horse" were to sow natural disasters and starvation across the planet. This graph sums up their efforts over the last forty years:

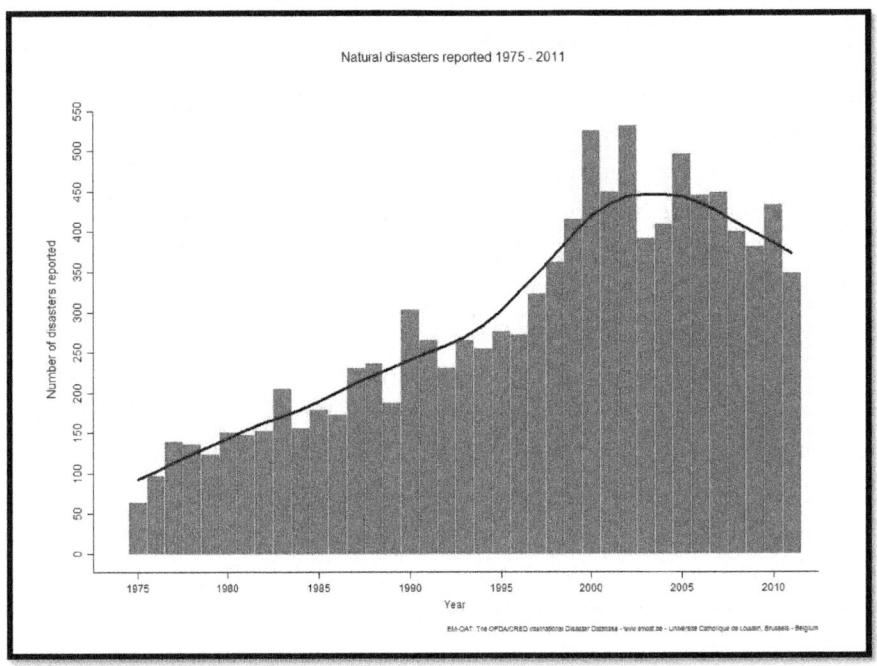

D. Guha-Sapir, R. Below, Ph. Hoyois. Natural Disasters Reported 1975-2011. 2015. EM-DAT: International Disaster Database, Université Catholique de Louvain , Brussels, Belgium. Accessed July 7, 2015. www.emdat.be.

This is worldwide data compiled by the Center for Research on the Epidemiology of Disasters (CRED). The graph depicts numbers of natural disasters in the world since 1975. These disasters include earthquakes, volcanic eruptions, hurricanes, tornadoes, blizzards, floods, tsunamis, landslides, avalanches, wildfire, famine/drought, and disease epidemics. CRED defines such disasters as ten or more people killed, one hundred or more affected, a state of emergency declared, or an international call for assistance made. While numbers of each kind of natural disaster ebb and flow over the years, we can see that even in the last forty years, the total number of natural disasters has risen from around seventy-five to over four hundred on average per year. That's an increase by 530 percent! Sure, we can blame some of this on global warming if we want, but it doesn't change the fact that God's Word predicted these things would come.

Lastly, while we haven't witnessed too many cosmic disasters as of yet, John displayed an eerie foreknowledge of very real cosmic threats that we worry about today. Before mankind had any clue what an asteroid was (let alone what one looked like up close), he gave an accurate description of one looking like a "huge mountain, all ablaze" slamming into the ocean (Rev. 8:8). He also described an epic solar flare taking place in our future, which will cause serious harm to mankind (Rev. 16:8-9). Something tells me he really saw these things in his vision and that they will come in due time. (And unlike a certain Hollywood blockbuster, this asteroid is going to win).

We can see that things are heating up in this world with conflict, killing, and disasters—they are all over the news. Jesus predicted that the whole world would be in anguish, perplexity, and terror over all these things happening before his coming (Luke 21:25-27). It's safe to say this is true in our present time. Not to be a "Debbie downer," but these things will only continue to get worse. The Horsemen are doing their job well in bringing judgment to the world.

THE PROMINENCE OF ISRAEL AND COMING OF THE THIRD TEMPLE

As these things come to pass, the nation of Israel will ever-increasingly become the center of the world's attention. One day, they will finally be able to rebuild the Temple of the Lord in Jerusalem (Isa. 60:13; Mic. 4:1-3) either through force of Zionism or by allowance of the nations. However, there will not be room enough for its original outer courts due to the "Gentile" hold on part of the Mount (Rev. 11:1-2).

Chapter 4 brought to light just how prominent Israel would become as it established itself as a nation once more. We could see prophecy conveying their significance and effect on their neighbors, but as we'll soon examine, Israel will become so prominent on the world stage as to receive the attention of all the world's armies. Even now, Israel is drawing the gaze of the world's nations for better or worse. Their conflicts with their Arab neighbors bring criticizing eyes from the UN, EU, the Arab League,

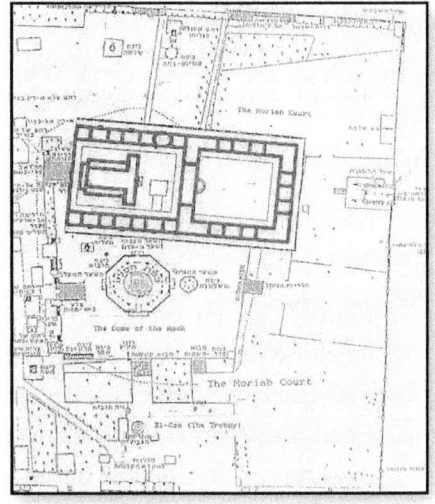

Temple Mount layout proposal blueprints. Option with temple next to Dome of the Rock mosque. Accessed March 12, 2015. Supportisrael.us.

and from leaders around the world. They are also forging new economic relationships with a number of world powers. We can bet that when Israel rebuilds the Third Temple, a large majority of the Muslim world will be in an uproar. This little country is making quite a stir and has potential to stir up much more.

As for the Third Temple of the Lord, both Old and New Testament make references to its coming:

➤ Isaiah described a temple being built after Israel's return from worldwide exile and rise to prominence (Isa. 60:1-13), so we know he couldn't have been referring to either of the first two temples.

➤ John described a vision of a future temple in Revelation 11—we know that he is speaking of a future temple because he is told that the land which was once the outer court of the temple will be under control of the Gentiles. The first two temples had outer courts. It just so happens that two Islamic mosques claim much of the land on the Temple Mount today. It makes sense that when Israel is able to rebuild their temple, they will have to concede some ground to the Muslims. (Take note of the temple blueprints above; newer temple designs do not include the large outer court area which used to enclose the entire Temple Mount.)

➤ Also, Paul foresaw the Antichrist coming to sit in the temple proclaiming himself as a god (2 Thess. 2:4). Since nothing like this has ever happened since his time, we must conclude that another temple will be built.

➤ Finally, Micah predicted that one day, people from all over the world would stream to the temple to see the Lord himself (Jesus) and learn from him. From this temple to come, the law of the Lord will preside over the entire world, and he will settle the disputes of nations (Mic. 4:2). Again, this can't happen unless another temple is in Israel's future.

All these things imply that there is a Third Temple on the way. As we've already learned, there are many in Israel who have been preparing for its return and would see it done. When the time is right, the Temple of God will be rebuilt on Mount Zion.

RISE OF THE BEAST

During these dark days, sometime after the temple is built, a league of ten nations will come together and give power to a dark and sinister leader known as "the Beast," who is also called the Antichrist. Satan will bestow upon this man great power and authority over the world. He will speak out against the Lord and the people of Israel, taunting and blaspheming them (Dan. 7:23-25; Rev. 13:1-8, 17:12-13). He will be fatally wounded, but when he survives, the world will be in awe of him, follow him, and worship him except for those who follow Jesus (Rev. 13:3-4, 8). The Beast will then exalt himself above all other gods and seek to magnify his power and glory in the world (Dan. 11:36-37; 2 Thess. 2:4a). A second "beast," known as the "False Prophet," will arise and aid him in this goal by performing supernatural signs of power to deceive the nations as to the Beast's divinity. This prophet will force the world to worship the Beast and a false image and to receive a mark of allegiance to him. Those who refuse will be killed (2 Thess. 2:9-10; Rev. 13:11-17).

Interpretation. The Beast, also referenced by names such as the "Antichrist", "lawless one," the "little horn," and possibly "Gog," is mentioned by several biblical writers. Both Daniel and John are clear that this individual will be given power by ten kings or nations (Dan. 7:24; Rev. 17:12-13). Many have speculated about whom these nations will be and where the Beast will come from, but there is no way to know for sure, yet. I believe the Beast to be "Gog" in Ezekiel 38 and 39, who leads the armies of many nations against Israel. Ezekiel described the same event as John when the armies of the world are to be led down to Armageddon by the Beast to face Israel and be destroyed by God (Rev. 16:13-16). Ezekiel described Gog as being a leader from the land of the "far north." If the Beast and Gog are indeed one and the same, it means that he will be the leader of Russia—the country farthest north of Israel. This makes sense in light of the current world situation.

In recent years, Russia has forged close relationships with Islamic nations such as Saudi Arabia, Iran, Egypt, Libya, Syria, Jordan, the Palestinian Authority, and others—all who hate Israel. Who better to be selected by the nations of Islam to lead them against Israel than their biggest, most powerful supporter? This is speculation, of course, but not unrealistic.

We will know the Beast for sure when he is mortally wounded then miraculously healed. After this, people would definitely take serious notice of him. Add in signs and wonders being done in his name, and people will start to see him as divine. He will then be given authority over all nations and seek worship from them (Rev. 13:7-8). When this one world government is formed, he will force people to wear his "mark" in order for them to be able to buy or sell anything. This idea has already come to reality, as people are starting to implant microchips in themselves to do just that, among many other things. It's voluntary implantation for now, but what John described as "the mark of the Beast" is already very attainable technologically.

Timing. According to Paul, the Beast will come to sit in the Temple of God, which Daniel supports when he said that this king will establish himself on the "holy mountain" (Dan. 11:45). This means that the Beast will likely come to power after the temple is built. It is possible that the Beast will come to power because of the worldwide incitement caused by the building of the temple. Time will tell.

THE FALL OF JERUSALEM

The Beast will then bring the nations to wage war on the people of Israel. They will defeat God's Holy People and Jerusalem will be conquered. The city will be plundered and its women raped. It will be delivered into the Beast's hands for three and a half years and half of the city's people will be exiled (Dan. 7:25, 8:24, 11:41; Zech. 14:1-3; Rev. 11:2, 13:7). The Beast will then establish his rule from the Lord's Temple, where he will sit and proclaim himself to be God (Dan. 11:45; 2 Thess. 2:4).

Interpretation. With the growing anti-Semitism in the world, it should be no surprise that one day a force large enough to defeat Israel will finally come against her. The exact reason for this is attack is not clear, but two very powerful reasons come to mind: 1) When Israel rebuilds the temple, there are going to be millions of angry Muslims in the world screaming for revenge, and 2) The Israelites were extremely resistant to the worship of other nations' gods by the time Greece subjugated them. It was Yahweh and only Yahweh. When the Beast starts demanding worship from the world, it is almost assured that the Jews will refuse and bring his wrath upon themselves. Daniel 11:36-44 seems to indicate that Israel will not be the sole target of his initial rampage, but that he will bring his military forces against anyone who opposes him in order to solidify his power. No matter the reason, both Daniel and John indicate that the Beast will conquer and oppress Israel for exactly 3.5 years (Dan. 7:25; Rev. 11:2; 13:7).

Zechariah also speaks of this event when the nations shall come against Israel and capture Jerusalem specifically, exiling some of its inhabitants. We know this can't be speaking of any capture of Jerusalem in the past, because after this particular exile, the Lord himself will come to fight for Israel. This points to the battle of Armageddon, which we will get to shortly.

Timing. This attack will likely come soon after the Beast is given his power, because the amount of time for his authority coincides with the time that Israel will be under his dominion. It also needs to be after the temple is rebuilt because after the Beast conquers Israel, he will set up his rule from within it on Mount Zion (Dan. 11:45; 2 Thess. 2:4). Once the Beast conquers Israel, the 3.5-year clock starts ticking to the Second Coming . . .

THE TWO WITNESSES

During this same time, two prophets (the Two Witnesses) will stand up in the captured city of Jerusalem. Empowered by God, they will call forth plagues of judgment upon the earth, and anyone who tries to kill them will be destroyed. Festering sores will break out on all people who have accepted the mark of the Beast and worshipped its image. The seas, springs, and rivers of the earth will be turned to blood, killing all that is in them. The sun will flare up and scorch the earth and its inhabitants, but they will curse God's name and refuse to repent of their sin and honor Him. Then the Beast's worldwide kingdom will be plunged into darkness—the people will sit in agony suffering from their sores (Rev. 11:3-6, 16:1-11).

At the end of these three and a half years of torment, the Angel of the Abyss will be allowed to kill the Two Prophets who wrought so much destruction and suffering, but ultimately for God's glory. The whole world will gloat over their carcasses and celebrate, but after three and a half days, God will bring them back to life and call them into heaven leaving the world in shock (Rev. 11:7-12).

Interpretation. Some believe that these witnesses are a metaphor for the Old and New Testaments, the church in general, or for something other than two literal prophets, but the evidence seems to point to the simplest interpretation. Revelation 11:4 refers to these two witnesses as "the two olive trees" that "stand before the Lord of the earth." This is a cross-reference to Zechariah 4, where the prophet sees these two olive trees in a vision on either side of a golden lamp stand, which held an oil bowl and seven lights. The angel says that the olive trees represent "the two who bring oil [for the lamp stand] and serve the Lord of all the earth (Zech. 4:1-14; brackets mine). Note that he was not speaking of "what" but "who"; therefore, the witnesses are actual people. Besides this, the context of Revelation 11 points to them being human—they can speak, call down plagues, they have physical bodies, and they will die and be resurrected.

It's interesting to note that when the prophets are killed, people from all over the world will be able to see their dead bodies lying in Jerusalem and will celebrate. This is now possible with television and the Internet.

The types of plagues which God will allow them to bring upon Earth seem to coincide with five of the "Seven Bowls of God's Wrath" poured out on the earth in Revelation 16, which means that these two men quite possibly will be the ones calling down these bowls. The symbolism in Zechariah 4 seems to support this idea, as they are the ones who bring the oil for the bowl on the lamp stand, thus implying that they are directly responsible for filling each bowl of wrath before it is poured out.

Timing. The Two Witnesses will appear once Jerusalem falls to the Beast (Rev. 11:2-3). Revelation 11:3 has them prophesying for the exact same amount of time the city will be under the Beast's control. The Seven Bowls of God's Wrath will come after the Beast has enforced his "mark" on people, as the first bowl is a plague targeting those who received it. At the end of the 3.5 years, the prophets will be killed, then resurrected; at this same time, the sixth bowl will bring the armies of earth together one last time against Israel. The seventh bowl will be poured out on the Day of God's Wrath—we know this because the events associated with it (the worldwide earthquake and hailstones) are the same events described elsewhere on the day of Jesus' second coming.

FORWARD UNTO ARMAGEDDON

The Beast will see that the people of Israel have been recovering from the previous war and that they have been living in safety and health from the plagues brought forth on the earth (Ezek. 38:1-9,14; Dan. 8:25). He will rage against them and once more reach out to the nations to bring an army down upon Israel like none other before assembled. Armies from nations such as Russia, Iran, Libya, Sudan, Ethiopia, Turkey, and many others will descend upon Israel in a great horde covering the land (Isa. 13:2-5; Ezek. 38:1-16; Dan. 7:21; Joel 3; Rev. 16:14). They will clash with the hopelessly outnumbered forces of Israel in a place called Har Megiddo (a.k.a. Armageddon, the Jezreel Valley, or Valley of Jehosaphat), which is northwest of Jerusalem (Joel 3:2,12; Rev. 16:16). It is there, in that wide open stretch of land, where the fate of the world will be decided.

Interpretation. First of all, we know that the "fierce-looking king" referenced in Daniel 8:23-25 is in fact the Beast of Revelation because of the context around his coming. He will "become very strong, but not by his own power," which fits with Revelation 13:2 where Satan is the one who bestows upon the Beast his power and authority. Daniel 8:24-25 connects with Revelation 13:5-7 where the Beast is described as proud and blasphemous toward God, and is given the power to defeat Israel. Finally, Daniel 8:25 says that this king will stand against the Prince of princes (another title for Jesus) and be destroyed by superhuman power—this happens to the Beast in Revelation 19:11-20. All evidence seems to point to this king as being the Beast.

This gives further evidence that Gog of Ezekiel 38 is the Beast, because in both Daniel 8:25 and Ezekiel 38:14, "Gog/the fierce-looking king" sees Israel sitting in safety after recovering from war and feeling secure. He then goes to war with them and is defeated by God. The connections are definitely there.

We know from earlier that God will allow Israel to be defeated and that Jerusalem will fall to the Beast for 3.5 years. During this time, the Two Witnesses will have been prophesying there and calling down

God's wrath upon the earth, ending with the Beast's kingdom being plunged into darkness (Rev. 16:10). Since Daniel and Ezekiel mention that the Beast sees Israel sitting in safety and security (Daniel mentions this after Israel's first defeat in v. 8:25), we can infer that the subjugated nation of Israel has been sitting back and watching God's wrath open up on mankind. They would certainly feel secure in the Lord if the rest of the planet suffers plague after plague while they live in peace, unaffected. Once the Witnesses are gone and the plagues cease, who is left to blame but the one bastion of light left on the planet . . . Israel.

Much historical debate has taken place over the identity of some of the nations whom the Beast will call against Israel (Ezek. 38). They are ancient names of tribes and nations representing modern-day places. Modern-day Iran was unquestionably Persia, and Cush is the old name for the upper-Nile region of Sudan/Ethiopia. Russia certainly seems to fit the bill of "Rosh" as the country to the far north. Josephus identified "Put" as Libya (Josephus, *A.J.*, 1.6.2). No matter whom they are, and research suggests that most of them seem to be Muslim nations who all pretty much hate Israel even today, there are going to be a whole lot of people angry at Israel for the suffering they just endured at the hands of God. Their hordes will descend upon tiny Israel near a city in their nation called Armageddon, or "Har Megiddo" in Hebrew (sorry, this time we're talking about a battle, not an asteroid). Several of the other prophets mention various locations for this battle throughout Israel, but let's face it—an army of the size we're talking about is going to be all over that country.

Timing. This battle will occur after Israel has been defeated in a previous war and subjugated for the 3.5 year period. Daniel, Zechariah, and John all mention this subjugation and that it will occur before Jesus comes to fight against the nations and the Beast (Dan. 8:25; Zech. 14:1-4; Rev. 11:3, 13:5-7, 16:16). As we have already seen, Ezekiel provides support for this as well.

THE DAY OF WRATH AND JESUS' SECOND COMING

Interpretation. There shall be no grander entrance in all of history than that of the Lamb on this day of redemption and wrath. It will be both awesome and terrifying at the same time. This is Jesus to the rescue of his people, plain and simple. Daniel tells us that the Beast (the horn) will be defeating the holy people, Israel, in this battle (Dan. 7:21). Throughout the Old Testament God allowed Israel to be placed in impossible situations like this so that they will realize they are nothing without God and cry out to him for help. And help he will. As the armies of the Beast rage against Israel, Jesus, the Messiah, will show up in awesome power and glory. This will be the moment of hope and victory for all of God's people, Christians and Jews alike, and it will be the moment of sadness and terror for those who rejected him and accepted worship of the Beast.

Those Christians who had died at the hands of the Beast will rise and join Jesus in the clouds (the first resurrection), followed by the Christians remaining in the world (the rapture). This is to spare them from the wrath Jesus will bring on the nations of Earth. The rest of the world will see Jesus come, the dead rise, and Christians all over Earth disappearing around them—they will mourn when they realize the truth and reality of it all. And, as I mentioned, so will the Jews. Then, all of heaven will break loose against the Beast and his worldly kingdom.

Timing. Many believe that the rapture of Christians will occur separately from Jesus' coming at Armageddon, before all the terrible judgments are poured out upon the earth, and before the Beast defeats Israel—this simply cannot be so from the order of events and context revealed in Scripture:

1. Jesus says that all the earth will see him come in power and glory when he raptures his "elect" [Christians] (Matt. 24:30-31; Luke 21:27). The rapture and Jesus' second coming are one and the same in these verses. Why would Jesus make himself known to the earth and then disappear again for several years? "Behold all my awesome power! I'm going to leave now . . . but I'll be back!" The world wouldn't bother worshipping the Beast after that once they realized the truth—the order just doesn't make sense. No, when Jesus reveals himself to the world, he's coming with awe-

some power and he's immediately going to put it to use against the armies of the Beast.

2. Jesus confirms that Christians will endure many of the judgments mentioned throughout the first part of Revelation and then, "At that time, they will see the Son of Man coming in a cloud with power and great glory. When these things begin to take place ... your redemption is near" (Luke 21:25-28). We know Jesus was talking about a future coming, not a coming during the tribulation of 70 A.D., because 1) he says these things will happen after the time of the Gentiles, and 2) 70 A.D. was a time of judgment against the Jews, not of redemption for believers and of Israel.

3. John also implies that Christians will be present during some of the nasty judgments God will visit upon the earth (Rev. 9:1-6, 13:8-10, 14:9-13), and in some of these cases that they would be protected. In other verses, John calls for patience on the part of Christians as they endure the Beast's persecution and judgments upon those who worship him (Rev. 13:8-10, 14:9-13).

4. John also confirms the timing of the rapture. In Rev. 14:14-20, he says that Jesus will appear, the believers will be harvested, and then God's wrath will be brought against the armies of the Beast (this section is another reference to the battle of Armageddon). He reinforces this later in chapter 20 when he says that those who had been killed for not worshipping the Beast would rise to rule with Christ on Earth (the first resurrection; Rev. 20:4-6). This implies that Christians will be around to suffer at the hands of the Beast and that this resurrection will occur right around the time when the he is defeated.

5. Paul gives us a few more details. He says that when Jesus comes again, the dead in Christ will rise first, then those Christians that are alive at that time will join them (1 Thess. 4:13-16). Since we know that this first group of risen souls will only consist of those Christians who had died for refusing the Beast, the remaining dead are to come later (Rev. 20:5).

All these things must be taken in context together, as these Scriptures all overlap and point to one another. First, God will bring judgments upon the world and the kingdom of the Beast, then the Beast will come against Israel with all his hordes, then Jesus will appear. The first resurrection and the rapture of living Christians will occur in that moment, followed by Jesus' day of wrath against the Beast, his armies, and his kingdom.

The armies that stand against Israel and the Lamb will turn on one another. Rain, massive hailstones, and fire will fall upon them and across the entire planet. There will be no question that God has arrived (Ezek. 38:19-23; Zech. 14:4-5, 13; Rev. 16:18-21). Between the earthquake and the falling sky, people all over the world will hide from the Lamb, knowing that the day of his wrath has come (Rev. 6:15-17). As Jesus provides a way for the people of Israel to flee the battle, he will come with the multitudes of heaven and the remaining soldiers of Israel and lay waste to the armies of the earth assembled against them. The Beast will then be destroyed and cast into the Lake of Fire (Isa. 66:15-16; Ezek. 39:3-5; Dan. 7:11, 26, 8:25; Zech. 14:3-5; Joel 3:11-13; 2 Thess. 2:8; Rev. 19:11-21). The slaughtered dead will be so great around Jerusalem that the blood will cover the land up to six feet deep for 180 miles (Rev. 14:19-20). Afterward, all of the nations who fought against Jerusalem will be struck with a horrific plague in return for their wickedness—man and beast alike will perish (Zech. 14:12, 15). The kingdoms of the Beast will fall, and his reign will finally be over . . . the reign of Jesus will then begin.

Interpretation. Several prophets mention this epic earthquake at the coming of the Lord to fight for Israel (Isa. 29:6; Ezek. 38:19-20; Zech. 14:4-5; Rev. 6:12, 16:18). Ezekiel 38:22 and Revelation 16:21 both speak of huge hailstones falling on the armies of the Beast and the nations of the world. All the while, people all over the planet will be taking cover and trying to hide from the Lamb (Rev. 6:15-17). We see here again between Revelation 6:12-17 and 16:17-21 the tendency to approach the same event in different ways. We can see that the earthquakes in each of the chapters are of epic proportions, powerful enough to level mountains around the earth. All this to say that each of the chapters of Scripture speaking of the worldwide earthquake and hailstorm tie those Scriptures together as speaking of the same event. As you read through all these Scriptures, they are pretty self-explanatory about the wrath that will befall the armies of the Beast and on all remaining mankind for coming against Israel, God's people. This day will reveal God's zeal for justice in a way we can't imagine.

Timing. Revelation 16 places the earthquake after the massing of armies at Armageddon. Ezekiel 38:23 says that the Lord will make himself known in the sight of many nations during or after the earthquake, and Zechariah 14:4-5 describes Jesus setting foot on the Mount of Olives as it splits in two from the earthquake. This means that the earthquake will herald his appearance along with the hailstorm around the same time. The fact that the people of the earth will be desperate to hide from the face of the Lamb amongst the chaos of the earthquake (Rev. 6:15-17) also implies that he will have already made his appearance, accompanied by the earthquake and the hailstorm.

THE RETURN OF THE KING

Those of Israel's enemies who survive this great battle will return to the distant lands from which they came and proclaim God's glory to those that remain in the world—their eyes finally open to the truth (Isa. 66:19). Meanwhile, Satan will be banished for a thousand years (or, at least, a very, very long time), so that he will be unable to lead men astray (Rev. 20:1-3). Then Christ will establish his millennial kingdom on Earth, and those believers who were brought up to him on the Day of Wrath will reign with him over the rest of the earth during this period (Dan. 7:27; Rev. 20:4-5). Jesus will take up his rule in the temple on Mount Zion. From here, his law will go out into the world, and he will settle any disputes among the people or the nations. Peace will reign (Mic. 4:2b-3). The survivors of the nations will come to see the Lord on his throne, to worship, to bring tribute, and to learn knowledge and wisdom from him. Those nations that do not go to pay tribute to the Lord or celebrate the Feast of Tabernacles will be punished (Isa. 66:20; Mic. 4:2; Zech. 14:16-19). These will be the last days for the non-believers of Earth to accept Jesus as their Lord. But still, not everyone will . . .

Interpretation. Jesus will establish his kingdom on Earth after defeating the worst of evils and bringing judgment on all those who opposed him. Some interpret the "millennial reign" of Christ in Revelation 20 to be a symbolic, indefinite period of time for the "church age." They believe that this section merely implies that Satan has been bound up during the time of Jesus' church and will be unleashed at the end to wreak havoc. I believe any other interpretation other than a straightforward literal understanding of the text is unnecessary and taken out of context with the rest of Scripture. There are several reasons I believe that this thousand-year reign of Jesus on Earth is literal:

1. There is nothing in verses 4 through 6 of Revelation 20 to indicate that this is a metaphorical section of Scripture, so why try to dodge the straightforward meaning?

2. Revelation 20 clearly states that the Christians who will die at the hands of the Beast will rise from death to reign with Christ for a thousand years (v. 4). None of the events involving the Beast have occurred yet, and I certainly don't know of anyone who has risen from the dead to reign on planet Earth with a Jesus who has not yet returned. If these things haven't happened yet, then the "thousand years" cannot be descriptive of the church age, which we are in right now.

3. Peter clearly states that Satan is currently roaming the world looking for people to devour (1 Pet. 5:8); therefore, he has not been locked up yet, and has been active during the church age. Is there any doubt that Satan and his demons are working in the world today?

4. The prophets wrote of the Messianic Kingdom on Earth many times (Ps. 47; Isa. 11:4-9; Dan. 7:27; Mic. 4; Zech. 2:10-13, 14:9-

21)—just to list a few. Jesus will establish his kingdom on Earth after coming to bring judgment upon the nations. Some of these are very physical descriptions of future activities on a physical planet Earth. The various prophets describe this kingdom in such a way as to imply that people will still have a choice to reject Jesus or come and worship him on his throne, in the Temple of God, in Jerusalem. The new Jerusalem in Revelation 21 is described specifically as not having a temple; therefore, the prophets were speaking of this millennial kingdom of Jesus in the aftermath of Armageddon when the earthly temple will still exist. If the OT prophets describe this kingdom coming after the same events mentioned in Revelation, then why should we interpret John's version of it any differently?

5. It is because of these prophets that the Jews of Jesus' day expected that the Messiah would establish his kingdom on Earth. The last question Jesus' disciples asked him before he ascended was, "Lord, are you at this time going to restore the kingdom to Israel?" Meaning, "Are you going to free us and establish your kingdom on Earth as God promised to King David?" Notice that Jesus did not deny this would happen, but that it wasn't for them to know when this would take place (Acts 1:6-7). The kingdom of heaven is here now, in a spiritual sense through Jesus' followers, but one day Jesus will come to establish his kingdom in a physical sense having brought to himself millions upon millions of kingdom citizens already loyal to him.

Timing. Both Old and New Testament writers agree that Jesus' kingdom on Earth will take place after the great battle against the Beast. It will last one thousand years, and then Satan will be unleashed once more. Revelation 20:3 states that this will happen after *the* thousand years has ended—the passage is very clear on the time, and the original Greek gives us no reason to interpret otherwise.

SATAN'S LAST RAMPAGE

At the end of this millennium, after the earth has recovered from God's wrath and repopulated, Satan will be allowed into the world one last time to deceive many and weed out those who are not faithful to the Lord. He will take as many people down with him as he can. He will raise a massive army from all the nations once more and bring it against Jerusalem. This time, however, there will be no fighting against the Lord. He will consume the armies of the world with fire and Satan will be thrown into the Lake of Fire to join the Beast and his prophet (Rev. 20:7-10).

Interpretation. This section further supports the literal interpretation of Revelation 20:1-6. Jesus will rule on Earth for one thousand years, but it will not be "heaven" in the spiritual sense. After the events of Armageddon and the purge of all those who had worshipped the Beast, Earth will be severely depopulated. If Satan in this section is able to rally an army "like the sand on the seashore" after he is released, then the people of the world must have still been carrying on their lives and having children as normal for a very long period of time. One thousand years is plenty of time for the earth to repopulate its numbers, so Jesus' thousand-year reign makes sense as a literal interpretation.

Also, the fact that Satan will be allowed to deceive all these people and rally such an army means that there will be many who will still not accept Jesus as their Lord and Savior—even while he will be sitting on the throne in all his power. Satan already knows his end, and he will try to take as many down with him as he can. He will also be used as a tool to weed out the last of those who chose to not accept Jesus. No one can say that God doesn't give as many chances as possible for people to repent and choose him—a thousand years is a long time to try and redeem people to himself!

Many people of the earth will come to Jerusalem in rebellion to Jesus, but those who reject him will once again not be allowed to remain and will be thrown into the Lake of Fire along with Satan himself. Those who choose to be apart from God will get their wish, but they will have to live with eternal consequences.

THE GREAT WHITE THRONE OF JUDGMENT

After this, all the remaining dead of the earth will be called before the throne of Jesus in all his glory. Then they will be judged according to their deeds in life. Those whose name is not written in the Book of Life will be cast from God's presence into the Lake of Fire, the second death. This will include "the cowardly, the unbelieving, the vile, the murderers, the sexually immoral, those who practice magic arts, the idolaters, and all the liars." Those whose names are in the Book will partake in everlasting life with the Lord and all who follow him (Dan. 12:1-2; Matt. 25:31-46; John 6:39-40, 12:48; 2 Thess. 1:6-10; Rev. 20:11-15; 21:8).

Interpretation. Some believe that the Great White Throne will only be for non-believers, but this does not appear to be so. Revelation 20:15 infers that there will be those of this "second resurrection" whose names will be written in the Book of Life and spared. Daniel 12:1-2 supports this when he says some will rise to everlasting life, others to everlasting contempt . . . when the final resurrection and judgment happens, it would seem that all who were still dead will stand before the Great White Throne. Matthew 25:31-46 supports this as well; it describes both believers and non-believers being separated by Jesus on his heavenly throne.

At this point, the chance to choose Jesus or not will be over. The line will be drawn, and the remaining dead will come to account for their deeds in life before the Lord Jesus himself, for he holds the keys to death and Hades (Rev. 1:18). Those who believed in Jesus will rise to everlasting life, and those who did not will experience the Lake of Fire, or the "second death." Paul summed it up rather clearly:

God is just . . . he will punish those who do not know God and do not obey the gospel of our Lord Jesus. They will be punished with everlasting destruction and shut out from the presence of the Lord and from the glory of his might on the day he comes to be glorified in his holy people and to be marveled at among all those who have believed. (1 Thess. 1:6-10)

This isn't what people, Christians or otherwise, like to hear about: judgment, fire, and brimstone; but I'm not here to sugarcoat God's Word, only share what it says. God means business, and Jesus will be the only salvation from this final judgment. No matter the amount of books piled against you, if you truly accept Jesus as Savior and do your best to follow him, your name will be written in that Book of Life, and you will enter into eternity with Jesus and the Lord. But evil will not be allowed to prevail in God's eternal kingdom—it must be quarantined—so those who have rejected Jesus, who covers sin through his sacrifice, must remain separate from God, who is wholly good. If God is all things good, then what remains when separated from him cannot be good, and that is not a place where I want to be.

Timing. As we discovered earlier, there will be two resurrections: One at the time of Jesus' second coming, and the other after Satan's final defeat. Daniel 12 makes it sound like there will only be one resurrection, but it does not necessarily conflict with there being two—we just aren't given all the information. John clearly states in Revelation 20 that only those believers who had died during the time of the Beast and had refused to worship him will rise to rule with Jesus during his thousand-year reign (v. 4). "The rest of the dead did not come to life until the thousand years were ended" (v. 5). This means that there will be many believers who will not be resurrected into their new bodies until after Satan is defeated.

FORWARD UNTO ETERNITY

Then, the Lord Jesus will declare that he is making everything new. The old heaven and earth will pass away in fire, and a new heaven and earth will come to be. God will set a new Jerusalem on earth as his holy city. It will be the inheritance of all who have accepted Jesus as Lord and Savior. They will drink from the waters of eternal life, and the Lord will live among them and be their light. There will be no more death or mourning or crying or pain. All those who follow the Lord and his ways will be with him and reign with him for all eternity (Isa. 66:22; 2 Pet. 3:7, 10, 13; Rev. 21, 22).

Interpretation. This is the time to which all believers look forward—the establishment of Christ's eternal kingdom on Earth, which will be everlasting. While the risen in Christ will receive new, undying bodies, this will not be the final piece of God's redemptive plan. The old Earth, which is tainted with the sin of man, will have to go as well . . . and the heavens along with it. Jesus will remake them along with a new heavenly Jerusalem for all believers to call home. We will be a new creation, and so will our new existence . . . an existence fully free of sin and where it will finally be possible for all to freely follow and obey Jesus. It will remain this way because people will no longer have to worry about physical needs nor will they marry and have children (Matt. 22:30). It will not be necessary because we will all be focused on Jesus and his glory and love. All that live with Jesus will have already accepted him freely, and no more childbirth means that no one else will come along who might choose to reject him. Jesus promised everlasting life to those who believe in him (John 3:16), so we will finally, at this time, come into that promise and be with the Lord for all eternity.

APPENDIX 2: OBJECTIONS & PARTING SHOTS

Over the course of this book, I have made my case for the power of prophecy to show God's divine hand on the Bible. I have drawn connections between over fifty prophecies and the historical sources that reveal their fulfillment. Along the way, I have addressed various interpretive and historical concerns. But of course, no case is complete without hearing the other side. Just like any other approach to defending Christianity, there are plenty of objections and "spears" thrown at biblical prophecy. In this section, I will address some general protests about the use of prophecy to support the Bible's truth, and I will also deal with specific objections to some of the more important prophecies I presented over the course of this book. While there might be questions out there regarding prophecies I didn't mention, there are simply too many prophecies in the Bible to cover them all.

GENERAL OBJECTIONS

1. Prophecy—everybody's doing it, so why should special consideration be given to biblical prophecy?

Prophecy has been around since man started worshipping the divine. Everybody wants to know the future and many have claimed to be able to do so: Astrologers, psychics, palm readers, cult leaders, religious figures and texts—even weathermen, sportscasters, and stock-brokers. Many might think of Nostradamus, who wrote an entire book of vague, cryptic prophecies back in the 1500s. Does the prevalence of prophecy/fortune-telling over the centuries render the Bible's use of prophecy irrelevant to its truth? Not at all! It just means that we should be discerning of the truth and that the Bible, which claims to be of God, should stand head and shoulders above the prophetic noise with regard to accuracy, quality, and quantity of its prophecies (especially those already fulfilled in history). More on this below.

2. Doesn't the very existence of a given prophecy provide influence for self-fulfillment?

Certainly it can, and some biblical prophecies have undoubtedly influenced or will influence their own outcome. I've already dismissed this argument against Jesus, but I will examine a modern example. Many religious Jews want to build the Third Temple because Scripture both commands it and predicts another will be built. If/when it is built, one cannot deny that the existence of such prophecies influenced their own fulfillment. However, one cannot overlook all the other uncontrollable prophecies and conditions which first had to become reality in order to enable even the possibility of building a third temple.

The prophecies surrounding the destruction of the Second Temple and the following dispersion of the Jews had to come first. Can't have a third temple while the second is standing, after all! It is extremely unlikely that the Jews started a fight with Rome with the intent of having themselves slaughtered, their country leveled, and the survivors shipped off into slavery all for the sake of fulfilling Scripture. As part of this, they would have had to ask the Romans to politely take seven years to conduct the war, wait to conquer Jerusalem and destroy the temple until the war's midpoint, go against all their religious beliefs to request Titus to desecrate the Temple Mount, and also ensure that they would be specifically shipped to Egypt after the war. The Jews wanted freedom from oppression, not fulfillment of judgmental Scripture. All the prophecies of chapter 3 were fulfilled in spite of the desires of the Jews—no possibility or motivation for self-fulfillment here.

What about more recent events? Could the Jews have manipulated world events so as to fulfill the prophecies of chapter 4? Again, would they have wanted to? One of the major reasons they were given their country back was out of international sympathy for the Holocaust. Did the existence of these prophecies influence Hitler's rise to power at just the right time to persecute the Jews and ensure they got their country back exactly in 1948? It doesn't take a prophet to know that Hitler wasn't trying to help the Jews fulfill their Scriptures. I doubt the Jews today are very grateful for that help, nor would they have wished it upon themselves if they would have had the option to ask Hitler for it.

Are we to also think that the Jews manipulated the formation of the UN, which enabled them to have their country back? Highly unlikely. Neither will we find that the UN conspired to give the Jews their country because of prophecy that they would return to it. The Jews certainly hung onto the hope of a future country and temple because of ancient prophecy, but there are far too many uncontrollable factors which they could not have manipulated to bring these Scriptures to fulfillment.

Many of the Bible's prophecies dealing with Israel do not motivate or are beyond the possibility of self-fulfillment, yet they still happened. Even with those prophecies in chapter 4 that do motivate self-fulfillment—promises of military, economic, and agricultural prosperity and accomplishments—there is never a guarantee that world conditions would support fulfillment or that they all would come true in the exact fashion described, yet they have. So while the existence of a given biblical prophecy might influence people to fulfill it, most usually require the fulfillment of other prophecies or support of other events that are either undesirable or outside the possibility of manipulation. This implies a greater power moving behind the scenes to ensure fulfillment—someone who can see all ends and push things in just the right way to bring about his plan.

3. Couldn't many of the Bible's prophecies have been based on what was probable or deduced?

Some of the short-term prophecies perhaps, but so often the

prophets of the OT did not tell their kings or their people what they wanted to hear, so why would they have risked their lives time and again unless they knew their messages were from God?

Man can make many accurate predictions about the near future based on current data, patterns, and trends. Even some distant future events for things that are extremely predictable, such as astronomy. But what about specific world events in one hundred years . . . two thousand years?

I could say based on current data and patterns of past nations that one hundred years from now, the United States will have fallen apart due to corruption and war and possibly get it right. But to say that around the year 2115 an alliance led by China will invade, start a seven-year war, destroy all our cities (destroy Washington at the mid-point), decimate our land, kill most of our people, and ship all the rest of us into slavery and exile around the world—and get every detail right through mere deduction or probability—is very unlikely. To then say that we Americans will retain our national identity and that in the year 3993, we will be restored to our country without a fight under the leadership of a man named John, who will organize it as a single entity without states. After which, we will rebuild all our ancient cities (to include Washington) by the same names, defeat Canada and Mexico in combat, restore all our desolate land, and become a greater military and economic powerhouse on the world stage than ever before—and get each of these details right somehow through deduction or probability—why, this would be impossible for even the most educated of historians, analysts, or military strategists. Yet this is what the prophets essentially did in predicting the future of Israel when you take their writings together. I deduce that these prophets must have had divine insight to get all these things correct—luck or probability just isn't a reasonable answer.

4. Prophecy can be read into a text where there is none.

True statement! And some are guilty of doing so. This is why I have focused on prophecies which are widely regarded as such by both

Christian and Jewish scholars. For those that are not as well-known, I have provided justification for my interpretation. Everything in Scripture must be considered in context of other Scripture to include prophecies. Historical context is very important as well.

5. Couldn't numerous failed prophets have just been excluded from the Old Testament?

This is the idea that if we throw out a million prophecies, by default some will come true, and we can then make a religion out of those that become fulfilled. In like manner, some surmise that perhaps there were hundreds of other Jewish prophetic texts over the centuries which made claims about the future. Isn't it possible that the OT was just a compilation of those writers who somehow guessed things right and the rest got eliminated?

True, Moses laid out one simple criteria for determining true prophets of God—100 percent accuracy (Deut. 18:14-22). Even if there were hundreds of writings of failed prophets of Judaism (we have only a few apocryphal writings excluded from Jewish Scripture, not hundreds), there is one key fact that makes this argument irrelevant. Not only were the prophets of the OT 100 percent accurate about things they prophesied in their own lifetime, they were also correct about events which occurred hundreds and thousands of years later—as we've seen, their words continue to be fulfilled to this day! Once the OT was completed, any process of elimination stopped, and verification of their divine foresight is what we continue to see. The exclusion theory cannot explain this.

6. Can't predictive prophecy confirm other religions too?

Perhaps, if they can compare to the accuracy, quality, and quantity of the Bible's one thousand-plus prophecies. It is not my desire to target a particular faith, so I will speak in generalities about my research into prophecies of other religions. I encourage you to investigate further if you wish to answer this objection in more detail.

Many of the world's current major religions have at least some proclaimed predictive prophecy, but only in very small quantities compared to the Bible (less than one hundred). Some ancient, mostly vanished religions have larger quantities of prophecies written down in antiquity, but most were never fulfilled, inaccurate, or vague. Many modern-day religions' examples of prophecy are either vague, stand-alone prophecies that don't seem to serve much purpose in the bigger picture, or they are very near-future predictions that could have been self-fulfilled, deduced, or written after the fact. Some of these prophecies are from religions created by one individual of which one or more have indeed failed, thus nullifying their credibility. The prophecies of more mystical religions tend to be interwoven with clearly mythical histories that simply cannot be proven. Some religions even have prophecies of their own messiah-like figure, however, these individuals either haven't come yet or don't boast the immense historical support that Jesus has behind him.

Am I an expert on the prophecies of other faiths? Admittedly no, although I continue to learn. But it doesn't take much digging to discover that the Bible is beyond compare when it comes to prophetic revelation supported in history. Its prophecies beautifully weave together in large interconnecting themes that span centuries of prophetic writers (not a single individual). Together these themes have individual purposes as well as a combined purpose of revealing God's overall plan for the redemption of mankind as discussed in chapter 1. Many biblical prophecies are very specific, as we've seen, and refer to events hundreds if not thousands of years in the making. We would expect to see this if a timeless God really has been inspiring Scripture throughout history—he has the big picture; man does not. No other religious text that I have explored has such continuity and accuracy over a span of thousands of years.

7. What about failed prophecies? Don't they invalidate the Bible?

If we could prove beyond a doubt that a given prophecy has indeed failed, then that would pose a serious problem for the validity of that given prophet and potentially for the entire Bible. Let's examine a few commonly touted failed prophecies to see if the writer really did fail Moses' test:

Isaiah 17:1-3→The Fall of Damascus

"See, Damascus will no longer be a city but will become a heap of ruins. The cities of Aroer will be deserted and left to flocks, which will lie down, with no one to make them afraid. The fortified city will disappear from Ephraim, and royal power from Damascus; the remnant of Aram will be like the glory of the Israelites,' declares the Lord Almighty."

Many allege that this never happened—Damascus has been a prominent city in the Middle East for over five millennia and has never ceased being so to this day. This prophecy clearly failed! Or did it? What was Isaiah getting at? First, some context.

In Isaiah's day, Damascus was the capital city of Aram, a well-established kingdom to the north of Israel and Judah (Van De Mieroop 2007, 204). In 732 B.C., King Pekah of Israel and King Rezin of Aram joined forces and attacked Judah. Their king, Ahaz, appealed to Tiglath-Pileser III, king of Assyria, for help and brought tribute. Pileser obliged Ahaz and sent his armies into Aram and Israel. Assyria destroyed the small country, laid siege to Damascus, and eventually conquered it and slew King Rezin. Pileser deported all the survivors to other parts of Assyria and brought in some of his own people to settle there (Anspacher 1912, 48-52).

The prophecy fits the historical context well. It is clearly speaking of Aram becoming a remnant, its surrounding lands becoming deserted, and of Damascus losing its royal position (it was absorbed into the Assyrian Empire). All of these events are attested to have occurred in multiple sources. So did Damascus cease being a city and become a heap of ruins?

There are several issues we must address in answering this question. First, "no longer" does not mean the city was to become a ruin for all eternity, and nothing in the original Hebrew implies this. The phrase simply means that its status as a city will be removed after the described event (QBible 2015). The fact that it became a large city again later does not negate this prophecy. Second, the fact that people remained in Damascus after this event also does not negate this prophecy. Notice that Isaiah did not say that Damascus itself would be deserted, only that this would happen to some of the surrounding cities of Aram. Damascus lost its status as a bustling city for a time because it was devastated in the lengthy siege, its entire population was deported, and it was thereafter colonized by Assyrians. It was effectively demoted to a small town. It likely grew up again quickly under Assyrian rule because the local provincial government was established there (Anspacher 1912, 52). Third, while we don't have much evidence describing the city's condition after Assyria conquered it, it's highly likely that the siege left the city in shambles. This was the common result of any siege back then. Cities were often demolished, built over, and repopulated fairly quickly. Roman historian Cassius Dio reported that after Rome razed Jerusalem in the first war with the Jews, they founded a new city on top of its ruins (Cassius Dio, *H.R.,* 5.69.12).

While Isaiah might have used some hyperbole in this prophecy, through examination of historical events and Hebrew language, we can see that he did not fail to deliver. After Assyria finished with Damascus, the city as it was known for centuries was gone.

Isaiah 19:5-6→The Nile River will dry up

Isaiah declared this as part of God's judgment against Egypt:

> *"The waters of the river will dry up, and the riverbed will be parched and dry. The canals will stink; the streams of Egypt will dwindle and dry up."*

Since the Jews were first enslaved by Egypt, there has been conflict between the two nations. Like every nation who has been unkind to the people of Israel, God proclaimed judgment against them repeatedly throughout Scripture. Skeptics point out that the Nile has never dried up and continues to be Egypt's greatest resource to this day—see another failure! One moment . . . true, the event in this prophecy has never occurred in Egypt's past, but there is no historical timestamp in the text that limits the timing of its fulfillment.

If one takes a moment to investigate, they would see that we are watching this prophecy come to reality right now. As of 2012, 80.4 million of Egypt's population (96 percent) live along the Nile Basin out of the 238 million total people across eleven countries that share the Nile. Demand for the Nile's water continues to rise while the potential for increase in supply is extremely limited. It is estimated that by 2030, populations living in the Nile Basin will increase by another one hundred million, thus putting an immense strain on water resources. Egypt is by far the greatest consumer of the Nile's water, as it gets very little rain and relies heavily on the river for irrigation. Countries on the upper Nile, however, are taking a growing interest in the Nile's resources and are working on projects which will result in greater loss of flow downstream. Another major problem comes from the existence of numerous dams along the river. While these help with water storage and flood regulation, they are preventing sediment and its nourishing minerals from travelling downstream. This in turn is causing large amounts of erosion. (NBI 2012).

A 2012 report by the Egyptian Center for Economic and Social Rights states confirms that Nile pollution is on the rise and available water in Egypt is on the decline. Ever-increasing amounts of industrial, agricultural, and sewage pollution are entering the Nile. Egypt's water treatment systems are overloaded, and current estimates show that around 95.5 percent of Egypt's population is drinking untreated water. This pollution is causing increased levels of disease and death of fish as well as poisoning of water used for irrigation. The report also reveals that fresh water availability has dropped by 63 percent per capita from 1959 to 2012 and that by 2025, Egypt will likely be a water-scarce country with estimated population growth reaching 98.7 million (Bottoms 2012).

So in refuting another alleged failed prophecy, we in turn have on our hands another modern prophecy in the process of fulfillment. In fact, Isaiah's prophecy continues to predict that "Every sown field along the Nile will become parched, will blow away and be no more.

Fishermen will groan and lament, all who cast hooks into the Nile; those who throw nets on the water will pine away" (Isa. 19:7-8). These problems are developing right now. Egypt and the Nile are in for some very troubled times ahead, and Isaiah saw this coming almost three thousand years ago.

Jeremiah 43 & Ezekiel 29-30→Egypt will be defeated and destroyed at the hands of Nebuchadnezzar of Babylon

As we know, Jeremiah and Ezekiel were prophets of Judah before, during, and after the destruction of Jerusalem and subsequent exile to Babylon. They, like Isaiah, also had a few choice words of judgment for Egypt for their treatment of God's people. They both predicted that Nebuchadnezzar, king of Babylon, would invade Egypt all the way to the borders of Cush (Ethiopia), break the power of their pharaoh, defeat their armies, destroy their cities and temples, make off with their riches, and even take some of Egypt's people captive. Did this really happen?

While historians confirm that Nebuchadnezzar did clash with Egypt in Palestine on a number of occasions, skeptics love to assert that there is no evidence of his invasion and defeat of Egypt. The Greek historian Herodotus wrote of this time period about a civil war between Apries (a.k.a. Hophra) and Amasis, but never mentioned a Babylonian invasion of Egypt (Herodotus). It is well known that Egyptians were not fond of documenting their defeats, so it should be no surprise that Herodotus did not glean this information from them. But there are in fact some very powerful pieces of evidence that point to these events having occurred.

Josephus, while farther removed from the events, does make brief mention of Nebuchadnezzar's invasion in his work, *Antiquities of the Jews*. He tells of a sweeping Babylonian campaign through several kingdoms, which ended in Egypt's defeat. "Nebuchadnezzar ... fell upon Egypt, in order to overthrow it; and he slew the king that then reigned and set up another (Josephus. *A.J.* 10.9.7). Even more convincing, however, are contemporary accounts from Egypt and

Babylon, themselves.

At the Louvre, there is a statue of an Egyptian royal official, Nes-Hor, which bears an inscription attesting to Babylon's invasion. It confirms that an army from Babylon invaded Egypt and made its way as far south as Elephantine (near Ethiopia), where they destroyed the temple. It describes a great slaughter among the armies, and Nes-Hor claims he turned the Babylonians back before they reached the region of Nubia. The fact that Babylon made it that far south implies that they must have ravaged the entire Nile Valley along the way (Cox 1881, 401-403).

We also have a short firsthand testimony from Nebuchadnezzar himself. At the British Museum, there is a fragmentary cuneiform inscription written in his name, claiming that he went to Egypt in his thirty-seventh year (568 B.C.) and defeated the king of Egypt, "Ama" or "Amasis." The inscription also seems to imply that he carried off soldiers and horses. Several Babylonian inscription cylinders of Nebuchadnezzar were also discovered near an ancient city in north-eastern Egypt, further reinforcing evidence of Babylon's presence there (Hogarth 1899, 117).

These are two *primary* sources from those who were directly involved in the events these prophecies describe. I would like to point out that this evidence has been known about for over one hundred years, so the fact that this prophecy is still questioned shows lack of scholarship. More could be said about the details of these prophecies, and we may never have all the historical data, but it seems clear that Nebuchadnezzar really did invade and defeat Egypt. While Jeremiah and Ezekiel seemed to use hyperbole and war language in these sections, as was common for prophets to do, they did not fail in their predictions that God would bring Babylon to devastate Egypt as part of his judgment against them.

While there are other prophecies questioned by skeptics, I hope I've shown that most often such issues arise due to lack of quality historical research or in some cases lack of historical data entirely, which is merely an invalid argument from silence. I stand by my belief that the prophets of the Bible are 100 percent accurate, and I hope in dealing with these three common objections that those still doubting might give the Bible a little more credit before quickly dismissing its claims on prophecy and history.

8. How do we know if the prophecies of the Bible are 100 percent correct since some might be eternally pending and leave us never knowing?

True, a number of biblical prophecies can fall into this category, to include most of the book of Revelation and any biblical prophecy that seems to speak of apocalyptic events to come. How then can we trust that these things will really happen if we can't declare a prophecy false at a given point in time?

Because we can't take such prophecies in a vacuum, but in context with the rest of the prophecies of Scripture. First, the Bible has proven itself trustworthy so far in its predictions, which continue to find fulfillment to this day. And as I mentioned before, there are only so many prophecies in the Bible, and as they become fulfilled, they provide a countdown to the fulfillment of the final prophecies in the chronology of God's plan. So while me may not know the exact timing of all of them, we are repeatedly assured that we are getting closer to seeing the remaining prophecies fulfilled.

There will always need to be some measure of faith until Jesus returns, but all the evidence seems to indicate that this God of the Bible is a being of his word, and when he says something is going to happen, it does!

PARTING SHOTS

In this section, I will focus on a few additional objections to some of the more prominent messianic prophecies addressed earlier. I am a details person, and I like to make sure as many angles get covered as possible. Plus, prophecies surrounding the Messiah are the most important in Scripture and also tend to be the most controversial.

In Isaiah 52:13-53:12 the "suffering servant" refers to the people

of Israel, not to Jesus or any Messiah. (See chapter 2, pages 72-74, 82-83, 85)

The prophecies in this section of Scripture are widely considered to be the most obvious predictions of Jesus as the Messiah. The parallels between these words and Jesus' life are stunningly similar. Some, especially Orthodox Jews, try to take away the power of these prophecies by claiming they refer to the nation of Israel, not to the Messiah at all. It is true that other prophecies of Isaiah such as 41:8-9 and 43:10 do clearly allude to Israel as God's servant. Both of these verses clearly refer to a group of people in connection to the title of "servant." These have national scope.

However, there are references to this servant that do not paint servant-Israel in a very good light. Isaiah 42:18-19 describes servant-Israel as deaf and blind. This is very unlike the righteous servant described in Isaiah 52, 53, and elsewhere. We know from this later prophecy that Isaiah spoke of an individual servant because he describes how this servant will redeem Israel:

> *"Before I was born the Lord called me; from my mother's womb he has spoken my name . . . He said to me, 'You are my servant, Israel, in whom I will display my splendor'. . . he who formed me in the womb to be his servant to bring Jacob back to him and gather Israel to himself . . . 'He [God] says: 'It is too small a thing for you to be my servant to restore the tribes of Jacob and bring back those of Israel I have kept. I will also make you a light for the Gentiles, that my salvation may reach the ends of the earth'" (Isa. 49:1, 3, 5-7).*

Israel was certainly not sent by God to redeem itself, so what is going on here? This is where the connection between the two "servants" is made. These verses are clearly from the perspective of the Messiah sent to save and redeem the nation of Israel. The Messiah-servant here bears the title of "Israel" to symbolize his connection to them and that he was to be the perfect representation of what God intended the nation-servant Israel to be—a righteous light for God to the nations, but they were not. Matthew built on this theme throughout his gospel, showing parallels between Jesus and the experiences of Israel. Jesus succeeded in all the ways they failed at obeying and serving God. So whom is Isaiah 52:13-15, 53:1-12 referring to? The Messiah-servant or the nation-servant Israel?

Messianic Jew, OT scholar, and author Michael Brown provides some convincing insight as to how we know these verses must be speaking about the Messiah-servant:

1. This section of prophecy goes against all the promises of the Torah (Mosaic Law or Covenant) if it applies to the nation of Israel. It depicts the servant as acting "wisely," being "highly exalted," and God's wholly "righteous servant," yet this servant was despised, rejected, and punished. All of Torah clearly promises that if Israel as a nation follows all of God's commands and is truly righteous, that he would bless and protect them. "The thought of the people of Israel, as a whole, being righteous and yet suffering for their righteousness is totally unthinkable from a Torah perspective" (Brown 2011, 4.6).

2. Isaiah 52:13-15 says that the servant would be disfigured and marred, yet become highly exalted and revered by kings. While the people of Israel have suffered greatly over the years and attained respected status in the world today, they have never been highly exalted or worshipped by the kings of the world. Jesus the Messiah, however, fits this Scripture perfectly. (Brown 2011, 4.6).

3. At no point in Israel's history has Israel been a true "righteous servant" of God. Scripture certainly depicts otherwise, and modern Israel certainly doesn't fit the mold. In the case of this righteous servant, he was to be smitten by God because of the guilt of others, not his own (Isa. 53:4, 8). This description applies easily to Jesus, however. (Brown 2011, 4.6).

4. Isaiah prophesied that this servant's suffering and sacrifice would bring healing and redemption (vv. 53:4-6, 12). At no time in Israel's history have their sufferings brought healing and redemption to nations who afflicted them—such nations have often found themselves under God's judgment! A righteous

Jesus bearing the punishment of sin to redeem a broken world, however, does make sense here. (Brown 2011, 4.6).

5. I would like to point out a couple other aspects of this section of prophecy that don't make sense if the servant is the nation of Israel. First, unlike the earlier references to the servant as a group of people, the Hebrew wording of these passages clearly refers to a man (QBible 2015). Second, Isaiah says that the servant was punished and died for the sake of God's people, Israel. Does it make sense to say that Israel was punished and died for its own redemption? Of course not. Isaiah was clearly referring to the coming Messiah, who we know through other prophecies was to be Jesus.

Objections to Daniel 9:24-26 (see chapter 2, pages 77-81.)

→Nehemiah's exchange with Artaxerxes was not a decree

Daniel 9:25 marks the starting point of this prophecy with a declaration to restore and rebuild Jerusalem. True, Nehemiah chapter two, which documents the only instance of a Persian king granting permission to rebuild Jerusalem, does not record an overt statement to a national audience. However, I would like to point out that a decree, or "command," as it indicates in the original Hebrew (QBible 2015), can be oral or written and varied in audience.

Nehemiah records that King Artaxerxes sent him to do this task and that he provided written documents granting safety, resources, and troops. Such documents would obviously be considered commands from the king and would likely have announced the purpose of supporting the rebuilding project in Jerusalem. There is really no issue here. We may not have every detail, but this event was more than sufficient to fulfill the intent of the prophecy.

→The anointed ruler in these Scriptures refers to Jewish King Agrippa II, not Jesus

King Agrippa was the last Jewish-Roman puppet king over parts of Israel before its downfall during the Great Revolt. Some Jewish scholars assert that Daniel 9 points to him as the anointed ruler of this passage, since he ruled close to the time periods alluded to by the prophecy (Brown 2011, 4.18). There are some serious problems with this claim:

1. Daniel says the anointed ruler will be killed before the final seven-year period (The Jewish-Roman War), yet Agrippa II, being allied with Rome, survived the war and lived until around 100 A.D. Even if "cut off" in a more loose sense meant that this ruler would lose his kingdom, Agrippa certainly didn't, as he maintained his rule well after the war. (Jewish Encyclopedia 1906, "Agrippa II"). Either way, this cannot be him.

2. Agrippa aided the Romans against his own people in war, so why would he be accorded the honor of the title "anointed ruler" by a prophet of God?

3. The rule and death of Agrippa was of no great significance to God's greater plan, the events described in this prophecy, or the future of Israel. Why would this trivial figure in Israel's history be included in a very pivotal prophecy about Israel's fate? The death of Jesus, however, affected Israel and the entire world (Brown 2011, 4.18).

4. Agrippa's rule and death are meaningless to the purposes of the prophecy laid out in verse 24. Did his death or the destruction of Jerusalem and the temple bring an end to sin, usher in everlasting righteousness, or bring about the anointing of a Holy One? If these things were to have been accomplished by the end of the Seventy Sevens, then these are the two options. Neither fulfills these ends. But Jesus did. Jesus is the only holy one to walk this earth. Because of this fact, his death on the cross solved the problem of sin and allowed man to attain righteousness in God's eyes through acceptance of Jesus as Savior.

Ultimately, it makes absolutely no sense that Daniel's prophecy points to Agrippa II as the anointed ruler—there are just too many problems with this. Jesus, however, fits into this prophecy perfectly in chronology, character, and purpose.

→I'm still not sure about the idea of the Prophetic Years used in the calculation of this prophecy and others.

It makes sense that the writers of the Bible would use a common time system throughout since the Scriptures spanned thousands of years, going all the way back to the times when a 360-day calendar was used. I've already provided a precise example from Revelation, but was this the case in the beginning also? Indeed.

Genesis 7:11 tells us that the flood began on the seventeenth day of the second month. Verse 24 says the waters flooded the earth for 150 days. Genesis 8:3-4 places the end of these 150 days on the seventeenth day of the seventh month—exactly five months. One hundred and fifty days divides evenly into five 30-day months. Here we have solid evidence that the 360-day calendar system was in use by the earliest writers of the Bible. This supports the concept of 360-day prophetic years used in later prophecies over the millennia for consistency.

Objections to Psalm 22 (See chapter 2, pages 81-82.)

→Psalm 22 is not prophetic or messianic

This psalm of a righteous sufferer appealing to God for deliverance has long been held by Christians as prophetic imagery of Jesus suffering on the cross. According to the Gospels, Jesus even uttered the words from some of these verses while he hung there. As I've already mentioned, we know this passage was written by King David—it says so right at the beginning—but do these words make sense coming from his perspective or that of a prophesied Messiah?

It is quite a stretch to apply this passage to David's life in any way based on what we know of him. It would have to be an extreme use of metaphor or hyperbole to attribute these things to himself—not so with Jesus, who claimed to be Messiah and descendant of David. To drive this idea home as to whether or not this prophecy is messianic and not pertaining directly to David, let's take a look at the later verses in this section:

"But you, Lord, do not be far from me. You are my strength; come quickly to help me. Deliver me from the sword, my precious life from the power of the dogs. Rescue me from the mouth of the lions; save me from the horns of the wild oxen. I will declare your name to my people; in the assembly I will praise you. You who fear the Lord, praise him! All you descendants of Jacob, honor him! Revere him, all you descendants of Israel! For he has not despised or scorned the suffering of the afflicted one; he has not hidden his face from him but has listened to his cry for help. From you comes the theme of my praise in the great assembly; before those who fear you I will fulfill my vows. The poor will eat and be satisfied; those who seek the Lord will praise him—may your hearts live forever! All the ends of the earth will remember and turn to the Lord, and all the families of the nations will bow down before him, for dominion belongs to the Lord and he rules over the nations. All the rich of the earth will feast and worship; all who go down to the dust will kneel before him—those who cannot keep themselves alive. Posterity will serve him; future generations will be told about the Lord. They will proclaim his righteousness, declaring to a people yet unborn: He has done it! (vv.19-31).

Wow! God's deliverance of this righteous sufferer from persecution and death was to be so epic that the entire earth would hear about it and turn to the Lord and praise him. Generations yet to come would hear of it and proclaim God's glory. While David's name and story is known throughout the world, have entire nations turned to God because of his story? Hardly. Have entire nations turned to the Lord because of how he rescued Jesus from death? Absolutely! And at the time of Jesus' second coming, all the people of all the nations really will bow down before him, bringing this prophecy to its complete fulfillment. So unless David thought of himself so highly that his life would bring about these things, it makes far more sense that he saw this as applying to the future Messiah and king promised by God to come through his lineage.

→ Psalm 22:16 does not speak of crucifixion

So this prophecy does appear to be messianic, but is it really speaking about crucifixion? Some Hebrew translations say this verse reads, "Like a lion they are at my hands and feet," not "they piece my hands and feet." Christian translators just changed it to fit their purposes! Or did they?

The Septuagint, which was translated prior to Jesus' life by Jews for their Greek-speaking brethren, actually translated this passage as saying "they pierced my hands and feet." And the Dead Sea Scrolls, also from before Christ, utilized the verb "ka'aru," the root of which means "to dig out" or "to bore through." A number of later Jewish Masoretic manuscripts use this verb as well (Brown 2011, 4.25).

We can see then that the use of the word "pierced" was not a Christian fabrication—the oldest translations prove it was used by Jews. Even if the text did translate as "Like a lion they are at my hands and feet," lions have claws and teeth that pierce. Either way it says that terrible things are being done to this man's hands and feet, which is exactly what happened during a crucifixion. I'd like to point out that this objection, now refuted, ignores all the other direct parallels to a crucifixion scene, which are hard to deny.

FINAL THOUGHTS

There is so much more information out there on biblical prophecy, so I encourage you to continue seeking the truth behind them. I hope that in dealing with the above objections, I have been able to reinforce the validity of the prophecies I presented in this book and show that biblical prophecy stands strong against attacks. There are many other objections to prophecy we could discuss, but I would like to pose some parting questions for thought. How many fulfilled prophecies do we as Christians need to defend as true before one will admit the reality that there is more than lucky guesswork or conspiracy going on in the Bible? Sure, one can keep slinging questions at prophecy until they're blue in the face and keep the truth at bay, but there comes a point in any court case or argument where we draw the line and say, "That's a lot of evidence coming together—I think I have enough to make a rational decision." Where is your line? And if you always have another question to push the line farther away, then I would ask this: Is it really an issue with the evidence . . . or is it more a matter of the heart and what you want to be true?

REFERENCES

1. Alekseyva, Ludmila. 1983. "Jewish Movement for Leave to Israel." *History of Dissident Movement in the USSR.* http://www.memo.ru/history/diss/books/ALEXEEWA/Chapter10.htm#_VPID_22.

2. American Israel Public Affairs Committee (AIPAC). 2014. "Strengthen U.S.-Israel Strategic Cooperation." http://www.aipac.org/learn/legislative-agenda/agenda-display?agendaid= %7BD9F4B5E3-4883-4800-97FB-7D5655789AAA%7D.

3. Anspacher, Abraham S. 1912. "Tiglath Pileser III." New York: Columbus University Press. http://archive.org/stream/tiglathpileserii00ansprich/tiglathpileserii00ansprich_djvu.txt.

4. Archer, Gleason L., Jr. 1964, 1974. *A Survey of Old Testament Introduction.* Chicago: Moody Press.

5. Bard, Mitchell G. Jewish Virtual Library. 2015. "Ethiopia." http://www.jewishvirtuallibrary.org/jsource/Judaism/ejhist.html.

6. ---. Jewish Virtual Library. 2014. "Immigration to Israel: (1948-2013)." http://www.jewishvirtuallibrary.org/jsource/Immigration/Immigration_to_Israel.html.

7. ---. Jewish Virtual Library. 2014. "Vital Statistics: Total Casualties, Arab-Israeli Conflict." http://www.jewishvirtuallibrary.org/jsource/History/casualtiestotal.html.

8. Bender, Jeremy, Amanda Macias, and Armin Rosen. 2014. "The Most Powerful Militaries In The Middle East." *Business Insider.* http://www.businessinsider.com/most-powerful-militaries-in-the-middle-east-2014-8#no-1-israel-16.

9. Bottoms, Isabel. 2012. "Water Pollution in Egypt: Causes and Concerns." Egyptian Center for Economic and Social Rights. http://ecesr.org/wp-content/uploads/ 2015/06/ECESR-Water-Polllution-En.pdf.

10. Brown, Michael L. 2011. *Answering Jewish Objections to Jesus.* Vol. 3. Ebook. Grand Rapids, MI: Baker Books.

11. Bunson, Matthew. 2002. *Encyclopedia of the Roman Empire, Revised Edition.* New York: Facts On File, Inc.

12. Cambridge Digital Library. *Mishna.* University of Cambridge. http://cudl.lib.cam.ac.uk/view/MS-ADD-00470-00001/1.

13. Cassius Dio. ca. 211-233. *Historia Romana* (History of Rome). http://www.gutenberg.org/files/10890/10890-h/10890-h.htm#b69.

14. Cavendish, Richard. 1998. "Foundation of the State of Israel." *History Today*, Vol 48, Issue 5. http://www.historytoday.com/richard-cavendish/foundation-state-israel.

15. Central Bureau of Statistics (CBS). "Tourist Arrivals, By Country of Citizenship." http://cbs.gov.il/publications14/1546_tayarut_2012/pdf/t04.pdf.

16. ---. "Income From Tourism and Expenditure of Israelis Travelling Abroad." http://cbs.gov.il/publications14/1546_tayarut_2012/pdf/t23.pdf.

17. ---. "Trade Countries – Imports and Exports." http://cbs.gov.il/www/fr_trade/td1.htm.

18. Cotton, Hannah M. 1989. "The Date of the Fall of Masada: The Evidence of the Masada Papyri." *Journal for Papyrology and Epigraphy,* Vol 78. http://www.uni-koeln.de/phil-fak/ifa/zpe/ downloads/1989/078pdf/078157.pdf.

19. Cox, Samuel, ed. 1881. *The Expositor.* Vol X. Second Edition. London: Hodder and Stoughton.

20. Craig, William Lane. 2008. *Reasonable Faith,* 3rd ed. Wheaton, IL: Crossway Books.

21. *Encyclopedia Britannica.* 2014. http://www.britannica.com.

22. Epstein, Rabbi Dr. I., ed. *The Soncino Babylonian Talmud.* Book II. Sanhedrin. http://halakhah.com/rst/nezikin/34b%20-%20 Sanhedrin%20-%2025b-45b.pdf.

23. Ewert, David. 1983. *From Ancient Tablets to Modern Translations: A General Introduction to the Bible.* Grand Rapids, MI: Zondervan. Quoted in McDowell, *Evidence for Christianity,* 50.

24. Guttman Center for Surveys of the Israel Democracy Institute. 2009. *A Portrait of Israeli Jews: Beliefs, Observance, and Values of Israeli Jews,* 2009. http://en.idi.org.il/analysis/idi-press/publications/english-books/a-portrait-of-israeli-jews-beliefs-observance-and-values-of-israe-li-jews-2009/.

25. Halley, Henry H. 2000. *Halley's Bible Handbook.* 25th ed. Edited by James E. Ruark et al. Grand Rapids, MI: Zondervan.

26. Hasson, Nir. 2013. "One third of Israeli Jews want Temple rebuilt in Jerusalem, poll finds." Haaretz. http://www.haaretz.com/news/israel/.premium-1.535336.

27. Hays, J. Daniel. 2010. *The Message of the Prophets.* Edited by Tremper Longman III. Grand Rapids, MI: Zondervan.

28. Herodotus. *An Account of Egypt*. https://www.gutenberg.org/files/2131/2131-h/2131-h.htm.

29. Hogarth, David G. ed. 1899. *Authority and Archaeology Sacred and Profane. Essays on the Relation of Monuments to Biblical and Classical Literature*. London and Aylesbury: Hazell, Watson, and Viney, L.D.

30. Irenaeus. 175–185 A.D. *Against Heresies*. Book V. http://earlychristianwritings.com/irenaeus.html.

31. Israel Export & International Cooperation Institute. 2012. "Israel's Agriculture." http://www.moag.gov.il/agri/files/Israel%27s_Agriculture_Booklet.pdf.

32. Israel Ministry of Foreign Affairs. 1997. "Conservation of Biological Diversity in Israel." http://mfa.gov.il/MFA/PressRoom/1997/Pages/CONSERVATION%20OF%20BIOLOGICAL%20DIVERSITY%20IN%20ISRAEL%20-%20O.aspx.

33. Jerusalem Institute for Israel Studies. 2014. *2014 Statistical Yearbook*. http://jiis.org/?cmd=statistic.500.

34. Jewish Agency for Israel. "New Aliyah–Modern Zionist Aliyot (1882–1948)." http://jafi.org/nr/exeres/192cd729-47b2-403b-b0a3-e6105dcb8463.

35. ---. 2009 "Aliyah Statistics 1948–November 2009." http://jafi.org/JewishAgency/English/About/Press+Room/Aliyah+Statistics/nov30.htm.

36. *Jewish Encyclopedia*. 1906, "Scribes." http://www.jewishencyclopedia.com/articles/ 13356-scribes.

37. ---. 1906, "Flavius Josephus." http://www.jewishencyclopedia.com/articles/8905-josephus-flavius.

38. ---. 1906, "Agrippa II." http://www.jewishencyclopedia.com/search?utf8=%E2%9C%93&keywords=agrippa+II&commit=search.

39. Jewish National Fund. 2014. "Forestry & Ecology." http://www.jnf.org/work-we-do/our-projects/forestry-ecology/.

40. Josephus, Flavius. 79. *Concerning the Jewish War*. Trans. *William Whiston*. 1737.

41. ---. 93. *Antiquities of the Jews*. Trans. William Whiston. 1737.

42. LaHaye, Tim, Ed Hindson, eds. 2006. *Exploring Bible Prophecy from Genesis to Revelation*. Eugene, OR: Harvest House.

43. Keren Kayemeht LeIsrael Jewish National Fund (KKL). "Trees in KKL–JNF Forests." http://www.wildflowers.co.il/kkl/english/search.asp?searchString=&color=1&type=2&family=1&x=28&y=5.

44. ---. "Turning the Desert Green." http://www.kkl.org.il/eng/forestry-and-ecology/afforestation-in-israel/turning-the-desert-green/.

45. League of Nations. "Interim Report on the Civil Administration of Palestine." 1921. http://unispal.un.org/UNISPAL. NSF/0/349B02280A930813052565E90048ED1C.

46. Levon Levy Dead Sea Scrolls Digital Library. "Learn About the Scrolls: Discovery and Publication." http://www.deadseascrolls.org.il/learn-about-the-scrolls/discovery-and-publication.

47. ---. "Learn About the Scrolls: Historical Background." http://www.deadseascrolls.org.il/learn-about-the-scrolls/ historical-background.

48. ---. "Learn About the Scrolls: Introduction." http://www.deadseascrolls.org.il/learn-about-the-scrolls/introduction.

49. ---. "Explore the Archive." http://www.deadseascrolls.org.il/explore-the-archive.

50. Lucian. 169. *Death of Peregrine.* http://sacred-texts.com/cla/luc/wl4/wl420.htm.

51. McDowell, Josh. 2006. *Evidence for Christianity.* Nashville, TN: Thomas Nelson Inc.

52. Mekorot: Israel National Water Co. 2014. www.mekorot.co.il.

53. Ministry of Aliyah and Immigrant Absorption. "Operation Moses–Aliyah of Ethiopian Jewry (1984)." http://www.moia.gov.il/English/FEELINGISRAEL/ABOUTISRAEL/Pages/ mivtzaMoshe.aspx.

54. Morris, Benny. 2008. *1948: The First Arab-Israeli War.* London: Yale University Press.

55. Nile Basin Initiative. 2012. *State of the River Nile Basin 2012.* http://sob.nilebasin.org/#

56. Oren, Michael B. 2002. *Six Days of War: June 1967 and the Making of the Modern Middle East.* New York: Random House Ballantine Publishing Group.

57. Paley, William. 1796. *A View of the Evidences of Christianity,* 2 vol., 5th ed. Quoted in Craig, *Reasonable Faith,* 340.

58. Pew Research Center. 2012. "'Nones' on the Rise." http://www.pewforum.org/2012/10/09/nones-on-the-rise/.

59. Pines, Schlomo 1971. *An Arabic Version of the Testimonium Flavianum and its Implications.* Jerusalem: The Israel Academy of Sciences and Humanities. http://khazarzar.skeptik.net/ books/pines01.pdf.

60. Pliny the Younger. 112. "Correspondence with Emperor Trajan." http://www.gutenberg.org/files/2811/2811-h/2811-h.htm#linknote-1068.

61. QBible. 2015. Hebrew-English Transliteration. www.qbible.com/hebrew-old-testament.

62. Rabinovich, Abraham. 2004. *The Yom Kippur War*. New York: Shocken Books.

63. Reinstein, Ziv. 2014. "2013: Record Year for Incoming Tourism." http://www.ynetnews.com/articles/0,7340,L-4475168,00.html.

64. Ronen, Gil. 2014. "Jews Pray on Temple Mount." Arutz Sheva. http://www.israelnationalnews.com/News/News.aspx/180325#.VL-paivF841.

65. Sales, Ben. 2013. "Ethiopian aliyah: Mission accomplished." Jewish Telegraphic Agency. http://www.jta.org/2013/09/03/news-opinion/israel-middle-east/with-ethiopian-immigration-over-obstacles-remain-in-integration.

66. Sharp, Jeremy M. 2014 "U.S. Foreign Aid to Israel." Congressional Research Service. https://fas.org/sgp/crs/mideast/RL33222.pdf.

67. Shelly, Bruce L. 2013. *Church History in Plain Language*. Nashville, TN: Thomas Nelson Inc.

68. Smith, Wilbur M. 2015. *The Incomparable Book*. Minneapolis: Beacon. Ebook.

69. Soffer, Ari. 2015. "Watch: Historic Practice Passover Sacrifice Held in Jerusalem." Israel National News. http://www.israelnationalnews.com/News/News.aspx/193464#. VWnwls9VhBc.

70. Suetonius. 121. *The Lives of the Caesars*. http://www.gutenberg.org/files/6400/6400-h/6400-h.htm#link2H_4_0006.

71. Tacitus. 109. *The Annals*. Book 15. http://classics.mit.edu/Tacitus/annals.11.xv.html.

72. Tourist Israel. "Nimrod Fortress." http://www.touristisrael.com/nimrod-fortress/6010/.

73. Twain, Mark. 1869. *Innocents Abroad*. Hartford, CT: American Publishing Company. http://www.gutenberg.org/files/3176/3176-h/3176-h.htm#ch56.

74. Van De Mieroop, Marc. 2007. *A History of the Ancient Near East: ca. 3000-323 BC*. 2nd ed. Malden, MA: Blackwell Publishing.

75. Vanderkam, James, Peter Flint. 2002. *The Meaning of the Dead Sea Scrolls*. New York: HarperCollins Publishers Inc.

76. Van Voorst, Robert E. 2000. *Jesus Outside the New Testament*. Grand Rapids, MI: Wm. B. Eerdmans Publishing Co.

77. Varble, Derek. 2003. *The Suez Crisis* 1956. Oxford, UK: Osprey Publishing Limited.

78. Voss, Carl Hermann. 1953. *The Palestine Problem Today, Israel and Its Neighbors*. Boston. Quoted on EretzYisroel.org. http://www.eretzyisroel. org/~peters/depopulated.html#2.

79. Wake Forest University. *The Gallio Inscription*. http://users.wfu.edu/ horton/r102/gallio.html.

80. Walvoord, John F., and Roy B. Zuk., eds. 1985. *The Bible Knowledge Commentary of the New Testament*. Wheaton, IL: Scripture Press.

81. Worldmark Encyclopedia of the Nations. 2007, "Greece." *Encyclopedia. com*. http://www.encyclopedia.com/topic/Greece.aspx.

82. Yaakov, Yifa. 2014. "2013 'record year' for tourism, government says." *Times of Israel*. http://www.timesofisrael.com/2013-record-year-for-tourism-government-says/.

CPSIA information can be obtained at www.ICGtesting.com
Printed in the USA
LVOW04s2350131015

457976LV00030B/122/P